TEACH
TO THE
TOP

AIMING HIGH FOR
EVERY LEARNER

MEGAN
MANSWORTH

First Published 2021

by John Catt Educational Ltd,
15 Riduna Park, Station Road,
Melton, Woodbridge IP12 1QT

Tel: +44 (0) 1394 389850
Email: enquiries@johncatt.com
Website: www.johncatt.com

ISBN: 978 1 913622 75 6

Set and designed by John Catt Educational Limited

Praise for Teach to the Top

In *Teach to the Top*, Megan Mansworth unpicks the misconceptions and the sometimes empty rhetoric applied to an ambitious curriculum. She argues that intellectually demanding work is an entitlement for all pupils, regardless of their starting points. And that if we are serious about turning high challenge from rhetoric to reality then we need to up our game in terms of our own subject knowledge. This book is beautifully written, full of great suggestions and underpinned by long-standing research. I shall be drawing on it in my own work and shall be recommending it to everyone.

Mary Myatt, writer, speaker and curator of Myatt & Co

How many of us have received feedback in observations that there needed to be more challenge for all? What does this even look like? Megan Mansworth's brilliant book, *Teach to the Top* is the book we have all been waiting for. This guide to all things high challenge explores why raising aspirations is so important and chunks research into easily understandable and useful golden nuggets. Through some brilliant metaphors, Mansworth cleverly argues the case for why we need to develop our own subject knowledge and consider more critically the way we stream and plan lessons for our students. After almost fifteen years in the classroom, I came away enthused and armed with practical strategies I could take away and trial in my own classroom. *Teach to the Top* is a game changer and it will have a huge impact on teachers and students alike.

Haili Hughes, author, Head of Education at IRIS Connect,
Senior Lecturer at Sunderland University

This book demands that we consider the educational experience that our students live out in the classroom, demonstrating how teachers can take steps to ensure that the nobility of their subjects endures. Megan Mansworth brings together both theory and practice to provide strategies for teachers who want to showcase the beauty of learning with students, shifting us further and further away from curricular dilutions and distortions of the past. A must-read for any teacher.

Kat Howard, Head of Professional Learning, DRET TSH and co-author of Symbiosis: the curriculum and the classroom

Contents

Acknowledgements

This book would not exist if it were not for the many excellent mentors, colleagues and friends that I have had the good fortune to work with during my career so far. From my PGCE to my leadership roles, I have learned so much from so many talented professionals – some have become firm friends, and some were in my life for a shorter period but were nonetheless a fundamental part of my teaching journey. I have not made a list of names because, firstly, it would be absurdly long, and secondly, I was worried about leaving anybody out! I hope, though, that you know who you are. Thank you.

Immense thanks must go to the wonderful team at John Catt Educational: to Alex Sharratt for believing in this book, and to Jonathan Barnes and Meena Ameen for helping to bring it to fruition. It has been a delight to work with you from my initial proposal to publication. Thank you all.

Thank you to my parents, Anthea and Kevin, who despite not having had the opportunity to go to university themselves, gave me so many opportunities and always made me believe that no form of knowledge was off-limits to me. I have always tried to provide the same self-belief to my students and I wouldn't be the teacher I am without you.

Thank you to Matt for giving me so much support, love and encouragement, and sustaining me with many dinners and copious amounts of chocolate while I was writing this book.

Most importantly, thank you to the many students I have taught, who have undeniably shaped my practice and the teacher I have become. It is an absolute privilege to teach young people and I have learned so much from all of you. 'Thank you' isn't enough, but it will have to do.

Introduction

What is teaching to the top?

'Teaching to the top' is an expression used quite commonly in teaching. It is not a new phrase or one of my invention. It's most likely an idea you first came across in your PGCE or school-based teacher training course or, if you are a more experienced teacher, one you have heard several times since then. It might have been a target scrawled on one of your observation forms when you were training or an idiom you've heard trip off the tongue of a senior leader. Before introducing what teaching to the top *is*, I want to address what teaching to the top *is not*, at least in the way I envision it. Hopefully, this will allow me to anticipate, at an early point, any criticisms of those who may not understand the meaning of the phrase or those who might have opened this book perhaps looking for something quite different to what it contains.

Teaching to the top is not – or, at least, should not be – an approach that prioritises the learning of a few students seen as 'more able' or 'higher prior attainers' whilst assuming that those with lower data or assessment scores need to be taught at a lower level. It is certainly not about labelling a select group of students as 'gifted and talented'. It does not categorise some students as being at 'the top' whilst others languish, by definition, at the bottom. It does not rely on ability streaming or separating students into groups depending on their attainment. Crucially, it is not an approach that is tied to just one pedagogical method, and which can only be used with one style of teaching.

So, what *is* teaching to the top? Put simply, the vision for teaching to the top I emphasise in this book is one of consistently teaching higher-level ideas and knowledge and making this accessible to all students in all our classes. Teaching to the top, when done well, is about teachers working to continually develop their subject knowledge, using and developing higher-level concepts in their curriculum plans and the classroom, ensuring that every student is afforded access to the most stimulating, challenging and thought-provoking learning opportunities. It is, in my view, a mindset that should underpin the way we teach, an ideology that should shape the way we conceptualise education, and a practical strategy for ensuring the richest, most productive educational experience for our students.

Teaching to the top is often used to refer to the idea of pitching lesson content at the 'top end' within a classroom to stretch and challenge a particular group, and then supporting students to reach that top end. Rather than directing your teaching at the bottom end and then 'adding on' challenge in the form of extension activities or additional work, the concept of teaching to the top, in its typical form, involves stretching and challenging all students to succeed by aiming lesson content at the highest achievers and then enabling everyone to reach that goal through scaffolding and differentiating by support. When advocating this approach in his book *The Learning Rainforest,* Tom Sherrington explains that rather than challenging only students at the top end with 'extras', learning happens best when teachers 'cater explicitly for the highest attaining students in any groups [...] pitching every lesson and the general thrust of every unit of work to stretch them' (2017:156). It is a strategy, then, that aims to ensure we are not holding anyone within the four walls of our classroom back, and which means that all students in our classroom are learning – so that no one is bored, frustrated, or failing to make progress.

Indeed, research studies suggest that pitching lesson content at the 'top end' is beneficial for every student; international comparisons of student achievement indicate that the highest performing educational systems have high expectations for all (Reynolds and Farrell, 1996). Consequently, in the classroom, teaching to the top – when the 'top' signifies the highest attaining students in the group – is, at its core, simply logical. If teachers don't teach to the top, then some students are learning nothing at all; some of the class are inevitably held back and restricted from making progress. Teaching to the top with high expectations for every child, therefore, is a demonstrably better and easier way of educating our students than aiming content at a lower level and then searching for ways to intellectually challenge our students beyond this point.

Within these pages, I will encompass discussion of this type of teaching to the top, and emphasise the value of teaching consistently in this way. Specifically, I will focus on the value of teaching to the top for *every* student in a class and make a case for the idea that every student in our schools deserves access to the same high-quality ideas no matter their prior attainment. I will discuss the many reasons why we should teach to the top in the classroom, and how to do it well, using both educational research and my practical experience as a teacher and leader to support the strategies suggested. However, I will also take the concept of 'teaching to the 'top' further than the notion of simply aiming our lesson content at the 'top end' of a group. Although this remains a conceptually sound way to think about lesson planning, I also aim to show here that the concept of teaching to the top can and *should* go much further than this. Further than the curriculum, further than grades, and further than data.

Reframing teaching to the top

By this I mean, what if we reconceptualise 'teaching to the top' as teaching to the *very* top? What if we imagine, in our Year 11 group, that 'the top' is a student in a university-level class? What if, when teaching Year 8 Set 5, we include concepts and ideas that we ourselves only learned a matter of weeks ago? What if we integrate Master's degree-level ideas when explaining a concept to Year 10? What if we ask difficult philosophical questions of our Year 9 students? What if we entirely reframe what we see as the 'top' in our classroom? What happens then? The simple answer is that great things happen with wonderful consequences for the quality of education in the classroom, teachers' enthusiasm and motivation, and students' achievement and enjoyment of learning.

This book will provide a research-informed exploration of the benefits of teaching to the top consistently while demonstrating how broadening what we as teachers conceptualise as 'the top' can enable our students to achieve fantastic results by granting them access to ideas, concepts and ways of thinking that challenge them academically and make university-level knowledge accessible. Furthermore, this book will explore how teaching to the top in the most ambitious sense of the phrase not only helps to spark students' enthusiasm for learning and to develop depth of knowledge and understanding, but can also encourage teachers to maintain, rekindle or increase their own passion for what they teach and the joy they take in their subject. A school in which teaching to the top is embedded in teaching and learning should also be an environment in which teachers are empowered to continually develop their own knowledge and to have this expertise valued and, accordingly, to share the extent of their own comprehension of their subject by persistently teaching at the very top of their intellectual understanding. I will show, therefore, how embedding a philosophy of teaching to the top in the classroom and across a department or a school helps to enable staff not only to continually develop their practice but also to *enjoy* developing their understanding and knowledge of their subject. Importantly, too, by 'understanding of their subject', I mean the subject as it is broadly conceived – as a rich and multi-layered discipline, rather than as a narrow set of GCSE-framed knowledge or a checklist of skills linked to assessment objective or examination requirements.

As someone who has worked in both teaching and academia, I aim to produce a text which is both practical and research-informed, bringing together my knowledge of educational research as well as my experience teaching and leading in the practical space of the classroom. To some extent, as well as being informed by research and practice, the book is also ideological because ideology cannot be removed from the argument that teaching to the top is critical in a system that values the role of education in achieving social justice for our young people. I hope that this ideology – one that aims for equity and social justice through empowering young people with knowledge that should belong to everyone – is shared by the vast majority of educators. Nonetheless, I do question some concepts and practices that have come to be unequivocally accepted by many in the education system without, perhaps, being subjected to sufficient critical and research-informed reflection, such as the prevalence of setting systems, the problematic notion of 'gifted and talented' or 'higher prior attaining' students and the imposition of set lesson structures or pedagogies on teaching staff.

You will find, within each chapter, several practical suggestions for teaching to the top in your classroom. These aim to provide some key strategies that may be applicable, but due to the breadth of the book, they are not intended as a 'pick and mix' of approaches that can be used in every setting or subject, but rather as examples of research in practice and as illustrations of how you might choose to apply the research. Since the application of educational research to the classroom is context-dependent, I also provide guiding questions to help you reflect – either as an individual or together with your colleagues, school or department – on the relevance of several points from each chapter in your own setting.

The book engages with discussions of pedagogy as well as subject content and curricula, demonstrating how the use of higher-level subject knowledge and teachers' ongoing work to develop their own academic understanding can be translated to the classroom in a wide variety of research-informed ways. However, in keeping with my valuing of context-dependency, my conception of 'teaching to the top' as it is envisioned in these pages does not privilege one mode of teaching and one pedagogical style. Teaching the top doesn't necessarily mean favouring one particular type of learning over another, but what it does mean is continually envisioning the opportunities, breadth and depth of our subjects by valuing the knowledge and understanding teachers can bring as academic experts in their subject. It means embracing opportunities to incorporate and apply that knowledge in the classroom, whilst academically stretching and intellectually inspiring our students as much as possible.

While I use a wide variety of research to support and develop the claims I make for 'teaching to the top', I am also guided by my own practical experience as someone who has been a teacher of English at secondary level. I also use my experience in a range of leadership roles – which have given me countless opportunities to observe, coach and mentor other teachers – to guide my observations, and the myriad conversations I have had with excellent teachers in my career who have shared their own experiences and methods for challenging students. Alongside this, I use my experience lecturing at university level, from first year to Master's level, to provide insights and ideas from university-level teaching and study which can also work to enrich learning and enable teaching to the top. I make no claims that every single idea or suggestion outlined here applies to *every* subject. I readily accept that my ideas are informed, inevitably, by my own ideological conception of schooling and philosophy of education. Each of us has such an ideology, even if this is unconscious and implicit. To a large extent, my own ideology is governed by a desire to provide access to the most challenging ideas, topics and concepts to *all* young people, and a belief that each individual in our classrooms deserves to be 'taught to the top' as far as is possible.

I aim to show that teaching to the top has phenomenal benefits for student learning, fostering a love for the subjects we teach, creating a school-wide culture of valuing academic knowledge and excellence, and even increasing teacher wellbeing. Above all, I aim to convince my readers that teaching to the top is what all our students deserve.

Chapter 1

Building the foundations: developing high-level subject knowledge

'We are not what we know but what we are willing to learn.' – Mary Catherine Bateson

It begins with your knowledge

You simply cannot aspire to the top for your students if you do not have a solid foundation of subject knowledge. You can't provide what your students deserve if you do not 'know your stuff'. To me, these statements almost go without saying, but a few times in my career, I have encountered the argument that teachers are, essentially, facilitators and that if you can teach, you can teach anything. I could not disagree more. Whilst you certainly don't need a PhD in a subject to be able to teach it well, and subject knowledge is not a magic wand that can make you a good teacher, it is nonsense to suggest that it is inconsequential. Would you like to go to university to be taught by someone who has only learned 'how to teach' and knows little about the subject? Or, to compare teaching to other professions, would you want to be referred to a dermatologist if your problem was gastroenterological? Would you engage a criminal lawyer to represent you in a divorce? The answers are so obvious that the questions seem ridiculous. In most fields, we tend to accept that expertise is specific. Teaching should be no different. It is true that no one can be an expert in everything, but we do need to *value* subject-specific expertise and recognise its importance in order to allow it to flourish and to enable us to use it to its full effect in the classroom. Just as it would be pointless and dangerous to be treated by a doctor who has a good bedside manner and listening skills but no grounding in the science of medicine, it is unhelpful to be taught by someone with a strong grounding in pedagogy but who is lacking the foundation of strong subject knowledge.

The importance of subject knowledge has been demonstrated in numerous studies. Muijs and Reynolds (2002) found that mathematics teachers with higher levels of pupil achievement in their classes tended to have higher levels of self-reported subject knowledge, while Coe et al (2014) found in their extensive meta-analysis of 'what makes great teaching' that the two factors with the most significant influence on pupil achievement were teachers' content knowledge *and* quality of instruction. 'Quality of instruction' (essentially pedagogy) incorporates strategies such as effective questioning and assessment – strategies that, arguably, in themselves require good subject knowledge. For instance, it is impossible to question pupils effectively if you do not know your subject well, as your ability to push students beyond their current level of understanding will inevitably be limited. Therefore, before thinking about embedding challenge in lesson planning, we need to start with ensuring our level of knowledge enables us to challenge our students. Essentially, subject knowledge forms the ingredients and substance of teaching. In much the same way as a chef needs quality produce to be able to create an amazing dish, a teacher cannot deliver a great lesson without the basic components of subject knowledge. Just as the chef needs to translate ingredients into something wonderful with their skills, so too do teachers need to bring to life the core content of their subject knowledge into learning in their classroom. To extend my somewhat clumsy metaphor, pedagogy is crucial too (no one wants a plate of raw carrots, after all) but, when it comes down to it, lots of different methods of teaching are possible, just as there are lots of different methods of cooking. On the other hand, no learning can happen at all if we have poor or inadequate core ingredients to begin with.

Those who have disputed the importance of subject knowledge have often cited Hattie's (2019) finding that teacher subject-matter knowledge had an effect size of 0.19, meaning that it was less effective than other factors like classroom management (0.52) or effective teacher feedback (0.75). Yet teacher subject knowledge is extremely difficult to measure. Studies of teachers' knowledge that find it to be relatively unimportant may, for example, rely on exploration of teachers' self-perception of knowledge (Sanchez, 2014) due to the difficulty of 'grading' teachers' subject knowledge in any clear way. Some teachers, therefore, might actually have fairly strong subject knowledge whilst being self-critical of their own level of understanding. Furthermore, other elements of teaching that have frequently been found to be impactful such as feedback (Gibb, 2004; Nicol, 2010) are likely to rely to a large extent on teachers having a good level of subject knowledge which provides the necessary starting point for identifying gaps in students' knowledge. The better our understanding of vital subject content, the better we will be able to understand how to sequence it over time and to pre-empt specific misconceptions pupils are likely to develop and how to overcome them.

A continual state of knowledge development

It is obvious to most of us working in the classroom that, when we know a subject well, we teach it better. Anecdotally, I have found that if you ask any teacher whether they taught a particular topic best in their first year or second year of teaching the subject, they will usually say it was their second. Speak to any teacher in a school about what topic they prefer teaching, and it is likely to be a topic they know well. This certainly doesn't mean, though, that a teacher with a First will be a better teacher than one with a Third, or that a Master's degree in your subject will automatically make you a better teacher. Learning is more complicated than that but, by recognising the centrality of subject knowledge, we ensure that we are continually developing, expanding and enhancing it and are able to steadily increase our ability to quickly incorporate the most advanced aspects of our own learning in our lessons. This applies whether you are an NQT following a prescribed scheme of learning or a head of department planning your department's curriculum offer. When teaching to the top, your knowledge and grounding in the subject are key to enabling you to devise challenging questions, helping you to plan at an appropriately high level, and giving you the tools to cope with the unexpected questions students might direct towards you. It also has the additional benefit of helping you to be a more confident teacher, which enables you, in turn, to inspire students with your excitement for the topic. If subject knowledge is fragile, it is difficult to have inner confidence, as to some extent you will always be worried that the 'mask' of knowledge will slip.

By prioritising subject knowledge development, we can also increase our own enthusiasm for our subject by engaging with it in thoughtful, intellectual ways – it is very difficult to be enthusiastic in front of a class unless we feel confident, calm and knowledgeable, and good subject knowledge enables us to be all those things. Feasibly, extending and developing subject knowledge may help us to rekindle our enthusiasm for the subject and remember why we became a teacher of that subject in the first place, which is wonderful because enthusiastic teachers may help students achieve better grades (Rosenshine, 1970) and teacher enthusiasm also increases students' motivation and interest in their studies (Patrick et al, 2000). In contrast, a lack of subject knowledge can lead to feelings of worry or insecurity. Giovanelli (2015a, p. 17) found that English teachers with a literature background, who were teaching A Level English Language for the first time, experienced emotions such as anxiety and a fear of not being an 'authority' in the classroom due to lack of knowledge. However, participants in Giovanelli's study also reported their own ongoing subject knowledge development through teaching English Language had a positive impact on their teaching more broadly. Teaching an area or a subject with which one is less familiar can be anxiety-inducing, but if we approach it as an opportunity to improve or develop, it can have hugely positive ramifications for one's teaching overall.

It can feel quite alarming to realise how central your own knowledge can be to your success in the classroom, as it really does mean that the buck stops with you as the classroom teacher. At the same time, it is extremely empowering to realise that developing deeper subject knowledge is always possible. We can always learn more. The exact form that subject knowledge development will take may vary depending on personal development needs and, of course, the subject in question but the key is that it should be ongoing. It is never 'done'. Rather than being a chore, this makes our job more exciting and dynamic; when we devote time to the development of subject knowledge, we give space to our passion for our subject and nourish our interest, thus making us ultimately not only more knowledgeable but more enthusiastic and confident (and consequently more effective) teachers.

Developing individual subject knowledge

So, the rationale for continual subject knowledge self-development by individual teachers is clear, but how do we address this in a practical sense? Teacher training courses such as PGCEs have often reiterated the importance of subject knowledge by asking trainees to engage in 'subject knowledge audits', which are self-reflective assessments in which students reflect on their areas of strength and development. It is a mistake to cease the 'subject knowledge audit' during the NQT year and, in fact, *all* teachers should be regularly engaged in a process of self-critically auditing their subject knowledge. This will then feed into aspirational teaching by enabling us to harness the power of that subject knowledge in our classrooms. It is true that, at first, reflecting on one's own areas for development on a subject level can be uncomfortable; developing deep subject knowledge can be intimidating and may even feel like an insurmountable task. However, if you are in a state of continually developing subject knowledge in a proactive way, your confidence naturally grows because you know you have a burgeoning knowledge base underneath the surface. That makes developing our subject knowledge to enrich our teaching incredibly exciting. If you are going to teach to the top, it is essential that before even thinking about embedding challenge, planning a lesson, or devising a scheme of work, you look at what you are going to be teaching and face the most challenging aspects of it for you, head-on.

Firstly, then, you might think about your own preconceptions about the topic: which aspect of the subject area are you least looking forward to teaching? This will almost always be the area you are least confident with and, therefore, the one you should address most urgently. After identifying your personal areas for knowledge development, you then need to take proactive steps to develop your understanding of key areas before teaching a particular unit or topic. For maximum efficacy, this should be broader than just focusing on the objective for one lesson. Before looking for practical resources for teaching – or, even if you have already had the lesson resources and plan provided for you – learn about the topic. This sounds incredibly obvious, but all too often, it is tempting to fall into the trap of going straight to a search engine and looking for teaching resources aimed at students, rather than learning about the topic itself in a more comprehensive and advanced sense. This is completely understandable, and I would certainly not advise 'reinventing the wheel' when it comes to creating resources if existing high-quality ones are available. However, it is very difficult to judge the quality of a resource or a teaching approach if our own subject knowledge is lacking.

Subsequently, for rich subject knowledge development, it is better to consult a richer quality and range of resources, including academic ones, to make sure that the level of your own knowledge significantly exceeds the level of the lesson you will teach. As a starting point (even if you are teaching Year 7), it's also helpful to consider what a university student might want to learn about a topic in order to feel confident and proficient in it. What books might they read? What material might they engage with? It is *much* easier to learn at a higher level than the one you need to teach at and work backwards from there, than to learn only to the level of the scheme of learning or curriculum point in question. You need to be able to know what comes *next* after the current learning to allow you to lay the foundations in the topic most adeptly, plan effectively, and gain self-assurance in your teaching. Furthermore, this strategy will enable you to respond adroitly to unexpected directions in the lesson and learning opportunities, which I explore further in Chapter 6. You will not share this with students all at once but it will be there, acting as a steady foundation to keep you secure. We should not only teach to the top but also aim to *learn* at the very top when it comes to developing our own knowledge.

Resources or means of knowledge development might include:

- Reading open access academic journal articles on the topic
- Reading academic textbooks; if you ask nicely, many university libraries will give free day passes to their alumni, or to teachers using the library for research

- Asking in teacher communities on Twitter for advice and recommendations on improving knowledge of key areas
- Following lecturers or academics on Twitter
- Accessing subject-specific journals for your discipline
- Subject-specific CPD
- Discussing the topic with colleagues (more on that below)

This requires a significant time investment at first but will pay off in the long run – both for you and for your pupils. However, although a rich level of subject knowledge is necessary, always remember that its development is an ongoing process; try to notice and reflect on what you learn from engaging with these sources, rather than feeling worried about the sheer amount of information available. It can also be useful to think about which elements of your teaching you could spend less time on, in order to carve out time for knowledge development. Which areas of your practice have limited impact, and therefore could be reduced? Could you spend less time on the design of your PowerPoint in order to spend more lesson preparation time reading around your subject, for example? If there is any element of your workload that could be reduced in order for you to spend more time on subject knowledge, it is absolutely worth doing, since – in most cases – subject knowledge will be the beating heart of your lesson.

Furthermore, while increasing subject knowledge in your areas of development is important, we can always learn in more depth about any area of the curriculum and then utilise this to inform our teaching and stretch our students. The more recent our research and learning, often the more interesting and inspiring our lessons will be. Even our areas of current strength can be developed further. We might fancy ourselves as something of an expert on Shakespeare, for example, but hearing about a new interpretation of a particular line in *Macbeth* can still enrich and enhance our teaching, and thus students' learning. There is no limit to subject knowledge development, and the very process of engaging with it allows us to continually reflect on our own learning and students' learning as well.

Subject knowledge as a communal endeavour

The crucial process of subject knowledge development should not only be an individual task, undertaken by teachers alone. While it is empowering and incredibly worthwhile to continually develop your subject knowledge as an individual teacher, it must also be a whole school priority. Yet myths that teachers should be prepared with all the required knowledge for teaching pervade education (Musanti and Pence, 2010); subject knowledge has historically been viewed as individualistic and fixed, whilst pedagogical knowledge has been emphasised as more complex and socially situated (Ellis, 2007).

This means that whilst in many schools a significant amount of time is devoted to whole school CPD in which pedagogical techniques are introduced and reflected upon, subject knowledge development may be a mere afterthought that is given meagre directed time. Leaders may assume that subject knowledge is the responsibility only of the individual teacher and is difficult to alter, whereas pedagogical skills are malleable and capable of change and development. As a result, schools may not devote enough necessary time to subject knowledge development, and compounding this is the fact that it often competes – in department-allocated time – with a raft of urgent practical considerations in the day-to-day running of the school, such as moderation of mock examinations or discussion of set changes. Yet this neglect of subject knowledge inevitably limits our ability to teach to the top, preventing us from challenging, enhancing or developing our own understanding of a subject.

We must find time and space for all teachers to engage in subject knowledge enhancement on a regular basis if we are to harness the immense benefits of expanding our own knowledge to enable us to teach to the top effectively and consistently. Prioritising subject knowledge development also has the benefit of demonstrating a trust in teachers and departments to effectively reflect on their own professional development needs, by giving them ownership of their own learning rather than imposing top-down pedagogical methods that won't necessarily work in practice, all the time, for all departments. Sitting through a lengthy CPD session on exit tickets or forms of AFL is unhelpful, for example, if teachers are not afforded time to reflect critically on applications to their own subject. Pedagogy is important, and nuanced reflections on pedagogy in our subject can be helpful, but ultimately teaching cannot only be 'research-based' (Wiliam, 2019) as teachers need to be critical consumers of research, reflecting on its application to different contexts. What works in one context will not necessarily work in another, and our subject is one of those contexts. Any whole school pedagogical policy should be undertaken in consultation with subject teachers and must be implemented only after carefully listening to feedback given from subject experts. Further to this, if leaders want teachers to improve then they should give them time to develop and expand subject knowledge – or, to enrich and improve the key 'ingredients' of our teaching, going back to the culinary metaphor with which I started this chapter.

Ellis suggests that the development of subject knowledge should be viewed as an active process involving teacher participation and proposes that the development of subject knowledge should be communal, a form of 'collective knowledge' (2007:458) developed as a group. She suggests we should be reconceptualising teachers' subject knowledge as complex and in a state of continual development, and highlights previous national projects which have aimed to help teachers develop subject knowledge in this collective way. For instance, in English, the National Oracy Project in 1987 (discussed in Johnson, 1994) and the Language in the National Curriculum project (Carter, 1990) were designed to promote the development of teachers' subject knowledge through collaborative work. In some schools and educational spaces – by no means all – our sense of subject knowledge as a continual process of development has been lost. In the practical space of our classrooms and departments, we can aim to regain this by engaging in collaborative work. As teachers, we should continually be learning – about how to apply our subject, about new developments in our subject, or by developing our knowledge in personal areas of weakness or lack of expertise. Shulman and Shulman (2004) put forward a vision of teachers as learners, helping to develop learning communities which have a common goal of development. Collaborative professional development can, in their view, bring us together. By focusing on the communal development of *subject* knowledge too, we can create collaborative learning communities with a focus on the inherent value of aiming for the top. Collaborative practices are crucial for effective professional development as by co-constructing knowledge, we can become empowered by it, rather than threatened by what we don't know. If we emphasise this conception of subject knowledge development, I would suggest that it becomes easier for teachers to form communities in which the pursuit of subject knowledge development becomes a shared goal, rather than something only *some* teachers feel they need to improve. These might even be termed 'communities of practice' (Wenger 1998:45) as teachers begin to form 'a community created over time by the sustained pursuit of a shared enterprise' – in this case, the shared enterprise being the development of deeper subject knowledge. This also allows us to harness the benefits of subject knowledge development, such as increased enthusiasm and efficacy in the classroom, on a communal basis throughout a school or department.

In practice, collaborative subject knowledge development might look like:

- Building in CPD time for teachers to share and develop their subject knowledge. The subject knowledge could be developed individually through reading, watching documentaries, listening to external experts, or attending subject-specific conferences, or any of the other methods outlined above; but crucially, there must be dedicated time for shared reflection, discussion and teacher-led presentation of learning.
- Working together to bridge the gap between the university and school iterations of the subject, for instance by discussing academic papers or articles together.
- Subscribing as a department to subject journals and using key articles as a basis for discussion.
- Spending a small amount of department budget on buying key texts to foster whole team enthusiasm for subject knowledge. These might be specific to key topics or schemes of learning rather than pedagogical texts, or university level subject texts.
- In secondary schools, having fewer whole staff meetings, and more time in subject-specific groups.

- Departments also might invest in collaborative CPD with specialist expert input in subject knowledge or an outside expert, as expert input combined with collaboration and peer support can be even more effective than purely peer support (Saxe et al, 2001; Harwell et al, 2001).

Owning and sharing our expertise

As well as reflecting on our areas of development, we need to recognise the expertise existing in our own departments that may sometimes go unrecognised. Alongside building in opportunities to develop collaborative subject knowledge, it is vital for us to value the existing subject knowledge around us in order to capitalise on departmental strengths.

None of us can be experts on everything, but in any department or school, you will have members of staff who are extremely knowledgeable about certain topics. For example, in a typical English department, you may have one member of staff who is an expert on Dickens, or on the poetry of William Blake, or in linguistics, or media, or another who is an amazing creative writer, and yet teachers may never be granted the opportunity to share this with others. We may spend years working alongside someone without realising their expertise in a particular area. In subjects such as science where teachers have studied one science specifically for their undergraduate degree, this lack of awareness of others' strengths might be less pronounced, but in many cases, we may have members of a team or school who have a deep level of subject knowledge in particular areas and yet have never been afforded the opportunity, time or encouragement to share this with others. Therefore, we miss out on an untapped resource in schools and have wasted knowledge in schools all over the country.

As a department (or, in primary schools, as a staff body), we should be regularly asking collective questions such as:

- Who are our experts on each topic we teach?
- Where can we find time for them to share their expertise?
- How do our experts in particular topics teach that topic?

By facilitating CPD time for our teachers to share elements of their expertise, we ensure that subject knowledge in the department as a whole is developed, and also recognise the valuable input that every teacher can contribute. This can also enable us to move away from a fixation on positionality, as even recently qualified teachers may have rich subject knowledge in certain areas that they can share with the department.

In practice, teacher expertise-led CPD might look like this:

- Teachers reflecting individually on the area that they are most confident with.
- Department leaders auditing this self-reflection and also noticing the expertise in certain areas of teachers who may be unaware of their strengths.
- After this process of self-reflection, leaders can set up a schedule of subject knowledge led CPD, with different members of staff leading CPD on high-level knowledge in certain subject areas each week. This does not have to be purely 'delivered' in a didactic way by the particular teacher sharing a particular topic, but can also involve discussion and collaboration.
- Teachers can then come back together at various points during the term to discuss how they have implemented any new knowledge. Importantly, collaborative CPD is more effective when spanning a significant period of time, as in at least one academic term, and should involve opportunities to reflect alongside time for trialling and input (Cordingley et al, 2003).
- For maximum efficacy, any new knowledge or departmental expertise should then be adapted into curriculum planning and can also inform collective approaches to planning and resourcing going forwards. (I explore ways of embedding challenge in the curriculum in more detail in Chapter 2.)

Being brave enough to make subject knowledge a whole school priority

Arguably, teacher subject expertise has not, in the last few decades, been recognised to the extent it deserves in our school system, whether from senior leaders who question your pedagogy despite not having a grounding in your subject, Ofsted inspectors under previous frameworks who saw fit to judge the quality of your lesson on a four-point scale while having little familiarity with the subject matter, or by a government who have, on occasion, imposed curriculum changes without sufficiently thorough consultation with teachers. Making space for teachers' subject-specific CPD takes courage. It requires senior leaders who do not expect to micro-manage every element of the professional development process. It requires us to trust in the self-reflection of our staff and a belief that we do not need to have the whole staff body in one room to believe that they are learning.

Finding this courage is necessary because teaching to the top cannot easily happen without having knowledge of sufficient richness and depth that it becomes easy and natural to stretch and challenge students in every lesson we teach. Subject-specific CPD facilitates this by prioritising the sharing and development of expertise which will ultimately enrich learning. Moreover, if students are going to value knowledge and learning, they need teachers who love learning themselves and they need schools that value intellectual challenge. They deserve teachers with a commitment to ongoing development of subject knowledge. This can be achieved with a school-wide commitment to continual subject knowledge enhancement which enables every teacher to be at the top of their game intellectually as well as pedagogically.

It also takes time as well as courage. It means minimising the amount of extraneous, low-impact administration tasks expected of teachers, and cutting down whole school CPD on pedagogy unless it is delivered with opportunities for teachers to reflect critically on its application to their own subject (or subjects, at primary level). We cannot in good conscience argue that we should 'teach to the top' without affording the same privilege to teachers themselves; to *learn* at the top of their competency and knowledge base in order to become both more inspirational and aspirational in the classroom. Excellent subject knowledge is an enabling force which allows you to become more autonomous, less constrained and, undoubtedly, a much more effective teacher. Fundamentally, learning 'at the top' and having top-level knowledge will enable you to teach to the top too.

QUESTIONS FOR REFLECTION

- How important is subject knowledge currently in your departmental, school, or individual development priorities? What are the consequences of this level of importance? Could you work to shift or change your CPD priorities?
- Are pedagogical methods imposed 'from above' in your school or department, or is there sufficient space and time afforded for subject-specific exploration of the applications of research?
- Is CPD in your school aimed at the 'top' or the 'bottom'? If you are a leader, is there any whole school CPD that can be adjusted or adapted to reflect subject-specific priorities, or even replaced with time allocated to departments? Are leaders in your school sufficiently reflective of subject teachers' expertise when attempting to impose top-down policies?
- How could you work to harness the expertise of individual teachers as experts in different subjects or topics in your setting?
- Do teachers have dedicated time for subject knowledge development in your setting?
- Are there opportunities for self-reflection and auditing of subject knowledge? If not, how could this be built in?
- Is positionality fundamental in your setting or are there opportunities for all to contribute? How could less experienced teachers be more empowered to share their subject knowledge in your school or department?
- Where can time and opportunities be developed for teachers to engage in subject knowledge development?
- Are there any extraneous, low-impact administration tasks you could reduce in your setting? What can you take away to allow room for subject knowledge?
- Do you see your own subject knowledge (and, by extension, other's subject knowledge) as continually developing or as inert and fixed? How could you adjust or change this?

Chapter 2

Embedding challenge across the curriculum: ideology and mindset

'Life is either a daring adventure or nothing at all.' – Helen Keller

An ideology of high-level knowledge in curricula

This book cannot contain an exhaustive list of high-level topics that a lesson, scheme of work, or year of learning 'should' contain. Given the breadth of the book and its applicability to a wide range of subjects, this would be impossible. There are already several excellent books for teachers on ambitious and coherent curriculum planning (Howard and Hill, 2020; Myatt, 2018; Robinson, 2013), which is therefore not the predominant focus of this book. However, what I wish to reiterate here is that the curriculum we choose to teach in our schools transmits a certain ideology. An ideology of challenge, an insistence that we should consistently teach to the top, needs to be embedded at the heart of our curriculum in schools. We need to consider both how we can lay the foundations for students' learning by linking to their prior knowledge, but also how we can include content, ideas and concepts that reach far beyond what others outside our classroom might believe a Year 7, 10 or 11 to be capable of grappling with. Challenge must not be an 'add-on' or an 'extra' in our lessons; it must lie at the heart of our teaching. This might be seen in our resources, in our vocabulary, in the questions we ask, and in our explanations but, at its core, teaching to the top lies in raising our expectation of what a child of a certain age or attainment level can reasonably be expected to do and understand. Partly, the design of a curriculum with challenge at its heart can be made easier by stripping away the need to mandate a certain *way* of teaching each topic, as these pedagogical decisions can be made by individual teachers as reflective and trained professionals. Instead, our focus should be on ensuring that challenging and intellectually stimulating content is embedded throughout the curriculum.

We can ask ourselves:

- Is the lesson content demanding?
- Is it, at the same time, accessible (with clear explanation, scaffolding or support)?
- Is everything geared towards one assessment or is learning broader than that in our curriculum?
- Which key disciplinary concepts will we begin to build early on and then develop in later years?

Linking to this, we also need to consider the balance we strike between breadth and depth of learning in the curriculum. The decisions made here will be specific to your subject, but we might reflect on ways – in our discipline – to ensure that students are exposed to a level of breadth in terms of curriculum content that will give them a rich understanding of the subject, but are also given the time to develop depth of understanding. Mary Myatt (2020) emphasises the importance of thinking carefully about which concepts, ideas and knowledge we prioritise in schools, as well as guiding students to consider how these link together. Challenge or teaching to the top does not simply mean cramming a curriculum full of content and getting students to revise this through repetition in preparation for external exams. Some schools misunderstand what is meant by a 'challenging' curriculum and take this to mean loading as much information as possible into their schemes of learning. Whilst a certain degree of breadth is necessary and useful, we should principally be thinking about what the 'top' might mean in terms of *quality* rather than quantity.

Depending on the subject, it may in fact sometimes be *more* challenging to spend more time exploring less content. For instance, a child may have a better chance of developing their ability to write a great essay by being afforded opportunities to draft, redraft and improve work. When introducing a new topic or concept, it may be easier to teach to the top if we slow down our delivery of content while increasing the challenge level. Challenge can also come in the way students are expected to *apply* learning (for instance, in the responses they write, and the examples we model) as well as the core content and resources themselves. Teaching to the top does not necessarily have to mean only utilising resources far beyond the capability of the class or implementing sweeping changes where previously successful topics or approaches are deemed useless. Instead, we can examine where existing topics the department or school is comfortable with can be extended and made more challenging in our future teaching. To take English as an example, some departments have responded to calls for a 'knowledge-rich' curriculum by only choosing core texts that are from the 19th century and are full of difficult vocabulary. While difficult texts can be a good way to increase the level of challenge in certain areas such as vocabulary-building, we can also 'level up' our challenge level by teaching difficult concepts related to our existing resources. For instance, the play *Blood Brothers* is an English Literature GCSE text on some specifications which is relatively easy to read but can act as an introduction to Marxist approaches to literary analysis, a starting point for deep philosophical discussions which lead to evaluative essays, lessons on concepts from English language study such as dialect and idiolect, analytical writing based on high-level model answers, or for understanding the key elements of tragedy. Simplicity of language, approaches or core concepts is fine as long as a resource or text is used as a vehicle to help students access more challenging ideas.

The process of deciding on which elements of high-level knowledge we wish to embed in our curriculum takes time and is – in itself – demanding. Consequently, I would recommend any reader to consult subject-specific texts on curriculum planning as well as the more general books cited above. What we mean by high-level knowledge and challenging concepts will also, of course, differ depending on you and your subject. Some ways to decide on what you, as a school or department, conceptualise as high-level knowledge might include:

- Discussing as a department which ideas you find challenging or are at the top of your knowledge base.
- Reflecting on concepts that students either find new and revelatory or perhaps difficult and thorny at first.

- Discussing high-level and *enabling* ideas or knowledge which can then feed through to later years of study.
- Discussing which elements of your own university study or broader knowledge could feed into the curriculum.

It would be a mistake to assume that we can simply swap a text, a topic or a resource and that challenge will inevitably follow. Developing a curriculum that aims 'to the top' in every way is a difficult process, but if curriculum planning is *not* experienced as challenging and thought-provoking, it is likely that not enough reflection is going into the process. The choices you make in your content planning will determine the richness of the educational experience that students encounter. These decisions, therefore, need to be approached with assiduous reflection on what a curriculum should contain, and why, and thoughtful consideration of what 'teaching to the top' means in every aspect of our curriculum.

A caveat to the ideology of challenge

On the other hand, as well as building our curricula around an ideology of challenge, we also need to consider what forms of knowledge we are giving to students. It isn't enough simply to state that a curriculum should contain intellectual challenge unless we specify the *type* of challenge. The choices we make about what children learn, and why, are often driven by ideological assumptions or philosophical concepts about a particular subject. We cannot avoid this, but it is vital to reflect critically on which ideas we wish to centralise in our curriculum. In English, for example, we might ask which authors and whose voices we deem worthy of study, and what conception of the subject our choices transmit to students. In history, we might ask which periods or events are most important for students to grasp and whose perspectives on those events should be emphasised. In science, we might reflect on how prominent contemporary concerns such as global warming should be in the curriculum, or in geography, which countries or events should be used as case studies and deemed worthy of study. What I mean to say is that while challenge should be central and teaching to the top must be our *modus operandi,* simultaneously we must not neglect broader questions regarding our philosophical position on our subject. By contemplating our own position in relation to the purpose of a subject at the same time as working towards an ideology of teaching to the top, we can ensure that we develop the curriculum in a consciously reflective way, and we embed the *right* kind of challenge for our subject. So, when developing a high expectation and high-challenge curriculum, we must ensure that we reflect on our own subject area while interrogating and exploring our own ideologies around it. When designing a curriculum, we assign value to certain things and implicitly dismiss others as less important. Such crucial decisions, therefore, need to be carefully justified and explored prior to implementation. Ofsted's sweeping statement that the curriculum should represent the 'the best that has been thought and said' (Department for Education, 2019b:10) requires a critical eye; the *best*, we might ask, according to whom?

It is important, therefore, that curricula are not only developed and implemented from the top down. Inevitably, examination requirements and the National Curriculum will have an impact on the curricula we develop, but it is also important when devising a challenging curriculum to engage in collaborative dialogue, debate and discussion prior to implementation. If teachers in our school or department are not given the opportunity to influence the development of departmental and school-wide curricula, we risk losing out on a plethora of valuable voices, experiences and contributions. Curricula are policy-informed but they cannot be viewed only as a centrally mandated, monolithic object devised by government and school leaders. They should exist in a continual state of improvement and development, and devising them should ideally involve multiple voices participating in a critical, shared and reflective process.

Fostering a collective mindset of challenge

When teachers have high expectations of their students' abilities, students are likely to have improved performance (Rosenthal and Jacobson, 1968; this seminal research is explored in more depth in subsequent chapters). Importantly, not only does teacher expectation have an impact on an individual class level, but teacher expectation as a collective staff body can have an astounding impact on student achievement as well. The notion of collective teacher efficacy (CTE) refers to the shared belief of a staff body in a school or educational setting that they can positively affect student achievement. First identified by Bandura (1993), CTE suggests that when teachers believe they have a combined ability to influence student outcomes, students are likely to achieve better results – a finding that has been reiterated in multiple studies (Goddard, 2002; Goddard et al, 2004).

Most significantly, John Hattie (2016) ranked collective efficacy as the top factor influencing student achievement in his extensive meta-analysis for his *Visible Learning* research. With an effect size of 1.57, CTE has been ranked by Hattie (2016) as a predominant factor influencing student achievement, twice as effective as feedback and teacher-student relationships and over three times more powerful a predictor of achievement than socioeconomic status. In other words, when we *believe* in our collective power to make a difference, we are much more likely to do so. Donohoo, Hattie and Eells (2018:42) phrase it thus: 'When educators share a sense of collective efficacy, school cultures tend to be characterized by beliefs that reflect high expectations for student success.'

This is highly relevant when it comes to embedding challenge in our curricula because it means that for teaching to the top to be most effective, the mindset of challenge needs to be embraced across a school. The concept of CTE tells us that we need to collectively believe and accept that *our* students in *our* school are capable of learning challenging concepts and high-level ideas, for them to be able to feel the same. Therefore, our goal must be to harness and nurture a united belief that we have the power to make a difference by developing and enacting what have been called 'high-expectation curricula' (Dudley-Marling and Michaels, 2012).

So, increasing CTE around challenge on a collaborative basis might include strategies such as:

- Setting high expectations as a whole school or department by having collaborative CPD and discussions around the elements of our curriculum and lessons that might be made more academically challenging. This should, ideally, take place in a discursive rather than via a top-down approach, in order to recognise the aspirational teaching already existing in the school. These discussions might be based on some of the research or concepts discussed in this book and could include questions such as:

- What are the most challenging concepts we currently teach?
- What does teaching to the top mean to us, as a department or a school?
- When have we taught challenging concepts successfully?
- Which topics might be pitched at a higher level or made more challenging?
- What ideas, knowledge or concepts have you heard other teachers teach and been inspired by?
- What ideas, concepts or challenges might our students benefit from being introduced to, and why?
- Are we teaching this topic in a way that we would be proud to be a student's first introduction to a subject if they go on to study this discipline at university?
- Who is particularly good at teaching particular areas of the curriculum 'to the top'? What could we learn from them? (This will, of course, be several different members of staff depending on the topic in question.)
- How can we ensure every student feels empowered to reach for the top in our subject?

- Facilitating paired or group supportive coaching, either within or beyond departments, where staff observe each other teaching with a particular focus on aspiration and teaching to the top. Staff can then come together to reflect on this on a whole school or wider basis. This is particularly effective if all teachers are involved and engage in the same process of self and peer reflection, from NQTs to senior leaders, in order to demonstrate that all teachers have the capacity to develop the extent to which they teach to the top.
- If you are a leader, try to use inclusive language around the potential of your team to make an impact; make them feel included in your goals in aspirational, high challenge teaching by sharing

this explicitly as a shared, inclusive endeavour. CTE suggests that teaching to the top should not need to be imposed on staff – and in fact, will not be successfully achieved if it is. Instead, leaders should work to make everyone in their setting believe in it themselves. This might take longer than simply telling people to teach to the top, but will pay dividends in staff buy-in and ultimately in ensuring long-term results.

Ongoing reflection on teaching to the top

Importantly, we should also build in space and time for reflection on the extent to which we are effectively teaching to the top and the impact of our high academic expectations. According to Donohoo, Hattie and Eells (2018:42) the key to building CTE is 'evidence of impact'; we must ensure teachers can see the *results* of a particular method in order to reinforce its usefulness or its value. They cite Bandura's concept of reciprocal causality (1993), which means that the more collective teacher efficacy we experience, the more likely we are to experience it in the future. In other words, CTE is self-renewing. The more we see the positive impact of our actions, the more we are likely to feel empowered to take positive collective action in the future. So we can build in reflective opportunities to observe the impact of teaching to the top by:

- Encouraging staff to share examples of student learning or challenge, for instance by voluntarily contributing videos or resources to discuss and reflect on as a staff body. (Note I say *examples,* not *evidence* – this should not be used as a tool to judge teachers but instead a means to reflect collaboratively on impact, and this message should be made clear to staff who choose to share examples of teaching to the top in practice.)
- Seeking out feedback from students on the impact of what they have learned. For instance, leaders can look for places where challenge is embedded, highlight this positively, and celebrate it collectively.

Departments can also come together after teaching, informally or formally, to reflect on the process of embedding this level of challenge. We might ask:

- How did our students get on with the topic/concept/idea/ curriculum content we introduced? (Note: a small level of initial discomfort is not necessarily a bad thing, as I will explore in Chapter 3.)
- Or, alternatively, have our students pleasantly surprised us by concepts or content that they were able to quickly grasp and utilise? What factors helped them to do this?
- What were our own sticking points?
- How can we make certain elements even more challenging?
- What aspect did we feel least comfortable in teaching?
- Which parts of our own subject knowledge would benefit from development, after teaching this topic?
- How did students apply the knowledge?
- How did high-level models work in practice? Did we need to scaffold these more? Do they need to be made more challenging?
- What were the key benefits and the key challenges?
- Is this a concept, idea or element you would teach again? If so, why?
- Was the scaffolding appropriate or not extensive enough?
- Where are students demonstrating a mindset of embracing challenge? How can we further increase this?

This collaborative process of planning for challenge and reflection can not only help departments to develop a strong positive sense of CTE but can also help us to avoid focusing on teething issues in a negative sense, instead using them as a point for development both individually and departmentally. Developing a mindset of CTE can also be helpful as part of the process of planning shared curricula and schemes of learning, enabling us to harness a shared vision of teaching to the top for every child in our classes.

Planning for challenge in the curriculum

A well-planned curriculum tends to be structured around acquiring initial understanding of concepts before then consolidating students' understanding (Fisher, Frey and Hattie, 2017). The same principle can be applied when teaching to the top; initial introductions of challenging concepts or ideas can sometimes be done in stages or revisited in order to embed them. When we engage in deep learning, we organise smaller pieces of knowledge into broader conceptual structures (Meta and Fine, 2019). Teachers can facilitate this by threading key high-level knowledge through the curriculum and building on the complexity of concepts as schemes of learning progress. Fundamentally, when we plan to teach to the top we use existing strategies for effective curriculum sequencing; we just aim this at a higher level. At the same time, though, teaching to the top is a consistent mindset, so any one-off resource or adaptation in our planning should also be pitched to the top.

Simultaneously, however, it may be useful to acknowledge how difficult it can be to teach to the top well and consistently. When planning a scheme of learning, it can be helpful to bear in mind the way in which it will inevitably be translated into your classroom setting. To help with this, we can think about the 'pedagogical content knowledge' (also known as PCK) (Shulman, 1986; 1987) each teacher needs in their classroom, a particularly helpful concept which refers to the knowledge teachers have of how to teach particular topics and to make their subject knowledge accessible to students. As teachers, we work to transform information and ideas into content that is 'pedagogically powerful and yet adaptive to the variations in ability and backgrounds presented by the students' (Shulman, 1987:15).

PCK might include, in practice, the strategies we use every day such as targeted questioning or providing feedback. When planning a high-challenge curriculum, it can be highly beneficial to consider, prior to the implementation, what the barriers to teachers' PCK might be. Leaders and curriculum planners can work to *anticipate* the tools teachers may need when teaching content at a challenging level and help them to prepare for this. All teachers already utilise pedagogical content knowledge continually, by using a range of strategies that we adapt to the learning needs of the individual students we teach. However, to ensure we 'teach to the top' and our challenging curriculum is effective, we can plan for the PCK that may be needed. In doing so, we can provide a bridge between the challenge of the material and concepts we introduce to learners and what they need to know and understand from the curriculum.

When planning a challenging curriculum that takes PCK into account, we might:

- Plan challenging questions and concepts into the curriculum to help teachers develop their PCK; give examples of potential deep or high-level questions in the curriculum plan.
- Provide or work together as a department to develop high-level model answers that are included with the curriculum plan as a resource. A pre-existing selection of excellent example answers or models will give both teachers and students the confidence to tackle challenging concepts, ideas or knowledge and to see how these can be enacted in practice.
- Embed key high-level vocabulary, concepts and ideas throughout, but also give examples and ideas of how these could be taught or used.
- Avoid making every task and lesson focused on the same form of assessment skill and ensure that the teaching of different areas is explicit in the curriculum.

As well as presuming difficulty, we should also obviously bear in mind that individual teachers may have greater knowledge of the subject area than the person planning the scheme of work, and therefore take feedback and ideas from them as well on how the curriculum might be made more challenging. When it comes to planning high-level questions, this does *not* mean directing more difficult questions at higher prior attaining pupils or providing add-on 'challenging questions' that students can answer as an optional extra. Being asked to think on a deep or difficult level, as well as encountering a range of high-level knowledge and challenging concepts, should be the right of *every* child in our classrooms, and we risk deeply limiting our students when we avoid doing this.

QUESTIONS FOR REFLECTION

- In what ways might collective teacher efficacy be increased in your setting? Of the strategies and ideas outlined above, which are the most helpful or applicable?
- Is there an ideology of challenge in your setting? If not, after reflecting on the ideas outlined above, what do you think could be implemented to alter this?
- Do you have a personal ideology of challenge? What does this look like in your own lessons? What do you think the impact of this is on the students in your classroom?
- What are your pedagogical content knowledge development needs, either as an individual or as a staff body?

Chapter 3

Thinking hard and challenging students conceptually

'The function of education is to teach one to think intensively and to think critically. Intelligence plus character – that is the goal of true education.' –Martin Luther King

Thinking hard

Ofsted has defined progress as 'knowing more and remembering more' (Harford, 2018), and it is true that facts and high-level knowledge can empower pupils. Teaching to the top can, partly, mean intrinsically appreciating that our students have the right to know what the word 'ephemeral' means even if they are in our bottom set Year 7, or that if they ask a question that relates to GCSE Biology in Year 8, there is no reason whatsoever why you shouldn't explain the answer to them. Provision of such information can be an immensely powerful way of opening new doors of knowledge for students that will enrich their understanding of the subject we teach. But just as we wouldn't expect to go to university and be handed a list of information simply to learn, teaching to the top cannot be distilled only to the facts that students remember in a knowledge retrieval quiz, or to the information we give them in a pre-printed knowledge organiser. Remembering information is certainly part of learning and retrieval practice on key information can ensure students remember it (Brown et al, 2014; Butler, 2010; Roediger et al, 2011). (Although it is worth noting that a study by Van Gog and Sweller in 2015 found that the testing effect decreases in efficacy as the complexity of learning materials increases.) Learning at a challenging level, though, needs to go further than this. We must also think about what students *do* with the information they are confronted with. In other words, are we able to give students opportunities to develop, discuss, and think deeply, in order to challenge them conceptually with the information we present them with?

The esteemed professor of education Robert Coe explains that thought is integral to learning: 'Learning happens when people have to think hard. Obviously, this is over-simplistic, vague and not original. But if it helps teachers to ask questions like, 'Where in this lesson will students have to think hard?' it may be useful.' (2013:xiii) When translating our challenging curriculum and high expectations to the classroom, we should reflect, therefore, on where the opportunities in a lesson are to 'think hard'. We might begin by asking the following questions when planning a lesson or a scheme of learning:

- Will students be given opportunities to think about the topic from different perspectives?
- Where could students be guided to critically consider the validity of an idea?
- Could we build in opportunities, at certain points, for them to formulate opinions and to express them? (I accept this is more relevant to some subjects, like English, than others.)
- Will the answers always come easily to students, or are there times when it might be more challenging? (I would suggest that the latter is a preferable scenario, as long as tasks are achievable, as I will explain later.)
- Where are students going to be encouraged to thoughtfully apply a concept to different contexts or circumstances?
- How do you judge and see whether the students are 'thinking hard' in your class?

Importantly, a calm, orderly classroom does not necessarily mean students are learning (Coe, 2013) and, when we make any aspect of learning too easy, we may risk actually detracting from learning in the long term. Bjork and Bjork's research on 'desirable difficulties' (2011:57) suggest that some strategies that help students to improve quickly can fail to lead to long-term retention, whilst creating challenges that slow down the rate of visible learning can increase retention in the long-term (Bjork and Bjork, 2011:57).

The research strongly suggests that it is good to find learning difficult – within reason. We may, in fact, be *more* likely to remember difficult concepts that we have had to grapple with, puzzle through, or work hard to understand initially than easier ones. This means that it is crucial that our students are presented with high-level information, tasks and expectations, and that while scaffolding and support are important, we must be cautious to balance this with challenge.

Struggling with no chance of success is not good for anyone, of course, but building small amounts of difficulty into learning can be highly beneficial. Unfortunately, there are no quick shortcuts to defining what type of task counts as a 'desirable difficulty', but they might include tasks that take longer to grasp and achieve or questions that require a level of deep, extended consideration. It is necessary to reflect critically on the subject you teach in order to really be able to state which sorts of learning tasks might be at the *right* level of difficulty to enable our classes to experience the appropriate degree of challenge. We should also be careful not to leap to conclusions about categorising a certain type of task or question as automatically 'difficult'. Bloom's taxonomy, for instance, is often used as a model for more challenging tasks or questions in schools, with some skills such as evaluating and creating viewed as 'higher order' than others, such as understanding and applying. It can be a useful tool for generating questions, but it could lead us to mistakenly dismiss the complexity of some tasks viewed as 'lower order'. Application of certain forms of knowledge, for instance, can be very challenging depending on the context and level of support offered. Similarly, simply understanding subject matter can require that students think deeply and critically in order to conceptualise new or challenging ideas. Equally, we should not presume that those tasks Bloom categorised as higher order will necessarily be more difficult (Case, 2013).

I would suggest that, in defining desirable difficulties in your subject, the following questions can be useful:

- Which aspects of the subject do we – as teachers – find most difficult to explain or to model? (These might also, therefore, constitute difficult elements of the subject for students.)

- Which aspects of the subject involve 'thinking hard' and how could these be embedded in lessons more regularly?
- Could any ideas currently introduced only at Year 10 or 11 or later be threaded through the curriculum at an earlier point? Can we look forwards to university or A Level study to find sources of a higher level of challenge that we could allow students to tackle at an earlier point?

When thinking about how we can get our students to 'think hard', we must remember that if background knowledge of an issue is lacking, it can be difficult to think about it from different perspectives (Willingham, 2008). Critical thinking may, therefore, be context-dependent and linked to the subject in hand, rather than a generalisable skill applicable to all subjects. We can address this by providing students with facts before then utilising these to facilitate discussion, meaning we build a conceptual understanding of a topic before using it as a springboard for deep thought. (Note that in Chapter 7, I discuss debate and dialogic teaching as a means of collective thought.) On the other hand, it's worth pausing to consider that, depending on the subject or topic, we do not necessarily always need to fill students' heads with knowledge, or front-load a lot of content, before we give them room to think. In English, for instance, the text can sometimes come first as a resource, without being framed by a teacher's analysis. Students' prior interpretations and experiences can provide a useful 'way into' study – this is the cornerstone of reader-response criticism – and the provision of too much extra-textual knowledge (Mason and Giovanelli, 2021:77) prior to reading texts may, in fact, constrain students' ability to develop interpretations and to make inferences informed by the language of the text. Similarly, in scientific subjects, teachers might conduct an experiment in front of students and ask them to work out what the experiment indicates, or in different humanities subjects, a striking or significant image might be provided and students given time to contemplate its significance in order to establish an important concept for the lesson. Thinking can occasionally, therefore, come before explicit teacher input and explication of key messages.

Planning for accessible challenge

Despite the value of occasional 'desirable difficulties' and opportunities to think deeply, teaching to the top should definitely not make learning feel generally difficult and unpleasant. Our students are unlikely to make good progress if they are unhappy and under-confident, as I will explore in Chapter 8, and so we need to balance challenge with accessibility. Whilst there are times when thinking hard is immensely useful for learning, we also want learning to be a positive experience for our students. Not easy, as such, but manageable and achievable.

We can achieve this by planning both for challenge and for how we will support students to access it – for example, by planning and developing flexible, optional scaffolds that enable students to reach 'for the top' in their learning. Such scaffolds might consist of:

- In essay-based subjects, providing key lists of academic phrasing and writing structures to help shape responses, so that students' focus can be on other elements of their writing.
- Pre-teaching or provision of vocabulary with definitions available to refer to.
- Explaining key concepts in several different ways, with clear examples.
- Dual coding to support understanding and memory (see Oliver Caviglioli's excellent *Dual Coding with Teachers* for a guide).
- Planning resources that will help students relate learning to their prior knowledge.

We can also make challenge accessible by clearly demonstrating the stages necessary to achieve something. So, when giving feedback, we should try to pitch it at a high level, but can provide clear demonstrations of how students can achieve the next step – for example, by using examples on a visualiser or providing clear models which show improved versions of work. Again, when we teach to the top, most of the time we are just using the skills of a good teacher but ensuring that this is at a challenging level.

Not only can challenge itself be made accessible but the beauty of teaching to the top well is that we are able to introduce students to challenging concepts, ideas and knowledge that will also simplify their future learning. When we teach to the top from the beginning, we lay the groundwork for success early. To use an example from English, I have frequently observed that Year 7 or lower attaining pupils are likely to be taught clunky phrases to frame their analysis of quotations, such as my least favourite line: 'I can see this in the quote when it says.' These phrases act as shortcuts to including evidence in writing and may initially seem like a simple route to quickly teach an exam skill. However, the correct academic way to introduce a quotation is either with a colon or by embedding it in a sentence, not with a clunky, repetitive phrase used throughout an essay. We shouldn't really need to use the word 'quote' or 'quotation' at all. There is absolutely no reason why a lower attaining or younger student cannot be taught to embed a quotation in the same way as a university student. Frequently, students are taught incorrectly just so that they can learn quickly.

While this may seem easier for the student at first, we then build a habit that is difficult to break and which has to be *un*taught before the Year 11 exams – and, unfortunately, often it isn't. By taking the time to model the correct way to include quotations in Year 7, we help to make students better academic writers for the rest of their lives. Conversely, a quick shortcut makes things easier at first and much harder in the long term. Students learn through spaced practice and repetition to do something incorrectly, and then we wonder why they can't achieve a Grade 9 at GCSE a few years later. This is just a small example, but you will probably be able to think of instances in your own subject when shortcuts can be counterproductive – a time when we might be tempted to aim too low in our expectations which means students have to 're-learn' how to approach certain tasks, consequently making learning harder on a long-term level. Teaching to the top from the start means that we don't have to undo any incorrect or misleading knowledge. Note that by shortcuts I do not mean *scaffolds*. The difference is that scaffolds support students to do something at a high or challenging level whereas shortcuts are an oversimplified approach that can restrict future learning.

The simplifying nature of complex concepts

By challenging pupils to think deeply, we can help provide a basis for further development or understanding of a particular subject or topic area, helping to build a schema that will later be enriched by further learning. Paradoxically, teaching students about ideas that are seen as conceptually difficult or even university level can even make it easier for students to understand ideas they encounter in the future. For example, I have regularly taught students from Year 7 upwards about conceptual metaphor theory, a theory from linguistics first outlined by Lakoff and Johnson (1980) in their seminal book *Metaphors We Live By*. Put simply, the theory states that we use metaphors to help us conceptualise and represent the world around us by 'mapping' concepts onto other ideas. For example, we can see the commonly used conceptual metaphor 'happy is up, sad is down' in everyday uses of metaphor such as 'that has given me a boost', 'cheer up', or 'he's feeling low,' and 'feeling down', to name but a few. Most people never hear about this concept until university level, if even then, and yet it is a highly enabling idea that facilitates understanding of the fact that metaphors are not mythical, mysterious parts of language, but are in fact inherent in the way we think and try to understand the world.

Of course, I don't give my Year 7s a complicated journal paper or a long university-style lecture on conceptual metaphor with lots of extraneous detail. But I do tell them about the theory in a simple way, explaining how it shows that metaphors are all around us, used continually in our language, and often represent the way we experience the world. Students then start to enjoy spotting metaphors in their everyday language, and they definitely don't get metaphor confused with any other literary technique. Learning about this broadens any student's understanding of what metaphor is, stops them from seeing it simply as an add-on term to help them get better marks, and enables them to realise that metaphors are used constantly in language and reflect the way we see the world. Rather than unnecessarily complicating metaphor, learning about this concept in a staged, simple way in fact makes understanding it *easier* and more accessible for students. The conceptual challenge is high, but once students have understood the idea, they are enabled to understand similar concepts in the future and to broaden and deepen their understanding of metaphor. They can spot metaphors more easily when they encounter them, and understand that metaphors are used constantly in our speech, rather than some esoteric technique only employed in creative writing. Once students understand the idea that metaphors are used all around us and help us understand and represent the world, they rarely 'forget' what a metaphor is in the same way as a child might who has only a superficial knowledge of similes and metaphors. Depth and intellectual engagement lead to remembering and, more importantly, to understanding.

This is just one subject-specific example, but it is clear that teaching to the top can enable students to develop a depth of knowledge that may seem surprising, but can ultimately enable them to build the foundations to understand and access more complex ideas in the future. The more challenging ideas that students have access to, the more they will be empowered to succeed and improve more rapidly as well as – in turn – to access more challenging ideas in the future by having built a schematic basis for their development. Ultimately, planning for challenge in the classroom starts with working to cultivate the mindset that students all deserve to be granted access to high-level ideas; in this way, we can avoid the pitfalls of taking shortcuts and pursuing the easier, but less intellectually productive, route. Teaching to the top is an ideology we enact in each lesson we teach, and if we take on board this ideology as we plan our students' learning, we ensure that students receive the education they deserve.

QUESTIONS FOR REFLECTION

- Where are the shortcuts (not scaffolds) in your subject?
- Are there any instances when you have seen shortcuts limit, rather than support, future learning? Where could you adapt your curricula or lesson plans to avoid this?
- Are there any 'simplifying' complex concepts in your subject? Could they be embedded within the curriculum at an earlier point than they already are, or in a more explicit way?
- Have you seen any examples in your own subject where students have learned something incorrectly through repetitive practice? Or any concepts they have misunderstood at an early point? How could you work to avoid this in curriculum or lesson planning?
- How do you build a balance between accessibility and challenge in your own lessons? Which strategies do you use that are useful? Is the balance right currently or could it be altered?

Chapter 4

Teaching to the top, not the test

'We aim above the mark to hit the mark.' – Ralph Waldo Emerson

The harmful consequences of grade-focused teaching

As teachers, it goes without saying that we want our students to achieve well and make good progress. Of course, this is by no means the only goal of a good teacher – wanting our students to develop a love of learning, for instance, is central for many of us – but it is a fundamental ambition that drives practice. Attaining high grades opens doors for students that might otherwise remain closed. Undeniably, a set of good GCSE results translates, in many cases, to opportunity, granting a wider range of choices to students in terms of the path they may go on to follow. Research from the Child Poverty Action Group has indicated that low GCSE grades have a direct impact on students' life chances, as well as being, perhaps unsurprisingly, more likely to be attained by students from less affluent socioeconomic backgrounds in the first place (Hirsch, 2007). Getting good grades is by no means an insignificant goal when it comes to helping our students achieve their dreams and pursue their chosen path in life. Who could blame any teacher for having the success of their students at the forefront of their mind? We have a moral purpose as educators and an obligation to ensure, as far as we are able, that our students succeed academically as well as flourish socially in school.

Beyond the importance of examination grades for individual students, there is also a cost to schools in failing to deliver exam results in the form of Ofsted inspections and other sanctions, and teachers are often put under extreme pressure to meet targets (Hutchings, 2015). Consequently, exam results are important not only for students but can also exert an overwhelming amount of pressure on teachers, many of whom are required to report grade-based feedback at regular intervals to senior leadership teams who themselves are working under the pressure of a data-driven inspection system.

It is no wonder, then, that conversations and references to grades form part of many teachers' interactions with students, particularly towards the later years of secondary school. Wilkinson et al (2020) found in their observational study of teachers' language in the classroom that references to grades were used both to encourage students to set targets to work towards, and also to distinguish between different students in the class and to give them differing goals. Therefore, model answers at high grades or marks such as 'Grade 9 level' may be shared with students, or checklists and success criteria of top-grade responses may form the backbone of many lesson plans for teachers who wish to teach to the top in their lessons. At first glance, this is logical. There is nothing wrong with helping students to understand 'what a good one looks like' when it comes to an examination response. And we may assume that regular reporting of grades and tracking of data can help us to 'close the gap' between high and lower-achieving students.

In fact, repeated explicit references to grades and marks can be counterproductive for students' achievement, even those capable of succeeding at 'the top' levels of achievement. Grades negatively impact student motivation (Chamberlin et al, 2018) and studies have indicated that provision of feedback without grades – as long as it is accompanied by concrete steps and points for improvement – leads to greater student progress (Butler, 1988). Repeatedly talking about marks, scores and using the language of grading may, therefore, negatively impact the achievement of students. Research also suggests that when aiming high is linked to grades rather than to high-level knowledge and academic learning, this can be harmful both to achievement and to self-esteem. For instance, a longitudinal study of parents' high aspirations for their children's learning in mathematics found that parental 'overaspiration' can hinder rather than help student progress (Murayama et al, 2016).

Also, what we see, define and judge as a 'Grade 7' or otherwise is relatively arbitrary, shifting up and down each year depending on grade boundaries. If we introduce the concept of what a 'Grade 6' or 'Grade 9' looks like too early in our students' learning journeys, we risk removing the joy and the point of our subject by making everything explicitly about the end result. When we teach students to aim for a certain grade too soon, we teach them that learning is about a destination rather than the journey. Often, in school, the criteria for formulating an excellent response to a question is quickly distilled to exam mark schemes with 'good examples' framed as hitting particular grade criteria. When students are approaching their final examinations, it is only fair and sensible to ensure that they are firmly aware of the criteria they will be assessed on, and I am not suggesting that the approach of self or peer-assessing using examination mark schemes or showing graded answers is unhelpful in all circumstances. It *can* be very valuable, but this should take place in moderation. While the occasional graded model answer may be useful and mark schemes can be a helpful tool, in some cases, we have allowed the language of the mark scheme or exams – rather than disciplinary knowledge of the subject or language around high aspirations in our subject – to underpin every aspect of the curriculum from Year 7 onwards.

If you emphasise the requirements of the GCSE from Year 7, you are likely to end up with exam-obsessed students who are not interested in learning for learning's sake, but rather, who ask in Year 10 or 11, 'Do we need to know this for our GCSE?' (I would go so far as to venture that a class who sighs and asks this when introduced to high-level knowledge may have been taught too much 'to the test' for years on end.) Exams and grades are important, but too often we let the exam become our guiding force from the very first lesson. We let our teaching be constrained and our ideas narrowed. Even the 'top' is not a very exciting place to be if it just means a top band answer on one aspect of an exam. Some secondary schools currently use versions of GCSE exams for assessing Year 7 onwards or plan Key Stage 3 curricula purely around GCSE assessment objectives. We must ask ourselves not only whether we are denying those students a broad education and providing only a narrow glimpse of what a subject offers, but also whether we risk eroding their interest and motivation and thus actually negatively impacting examination results. The same questions also apply to primary schools and the extent to which SATS determine curriculum content.

Aiming for the top, not the test

Paradoxically, the best way to help students to attain the highest marks possible might be to *not* explicitly aim for them at all. Bear with me here; I'm not suggesting that we aim for the middle, or that we don't aim for our students to achieve great things. The quotation from Ralph Waldo Emerson given at the beginning of this chapter encapsulates my own approach. We do not need to aim for a Grade 7, or 8, or 9 to enable students to get there. In fact, we should be aiming *even higher*. This frees us from the limitations of grade-based models and feedback, but at the same time allows us to ensure that students are equipped to attain the top grades anyway. Rosenthal and Jacobson's classic study (1968) and concept of the 'Pygmalion effect' suggests that teacher expectations influence student performance. Positive expectations influence performance positively, and negative expectations influence performance negatively. In other words, when we expect students to achieve fantastic things, they are far more likely to attain those goals and work in ways that make achievement more likely. So, to create a climate of success, we need to give students aspirational goals to work towards and they need to believe their teacher has faith in their ability to attain these goals, without being inordinately pressured to hit certain grades or marks. So, we can model answers, give examples, or share ideas with students at the highest levels, using the full extent of our own knowledge to help them achieve highly. This enables us to harness the benefits of high teacher expectations and aspirations without falling prey to the negative consequences of over-grading.

We can ensure students achieve amazing results by teaching to the *very* top – that is to say, aiming *beyond* the level of the highest grade by incorporating advanced concepts and knowledge in our lessons, such as from degree-level study or recently developed subject knowledge, as discussed in the previous chapter. Using this approach, we barely have to mention grades or the exam at all, except in the final run-up to assessments, because we are continually using excellent examples and sharing these with students. This method not only means students are likely to get even better results but also helps them to realise that learning has intrinsic value as well as being a tool for passing exams. By using model answers or example work from far above the target grade and beyond the curriculum or the examination, we free our students from a fixation on their 'current level' and inspire them to strive for that level of success. While they might not quite reach it, aiming for the top can help them get pretty close by the end of their final year. It also completely removes any necessity to continually refer to grading because, instead, we are simply striving for the best. When we set our sights on the highest levels of scholarship, the grades are likely to follow.

So, if you teach an essay-based subject and are writing a model answer, it doesn't need to be written to fit a particular grade. You can try just writing to the best of your ability and then simply exploring, with your class, why it is good. Once students aim for the same high level, they will achieve something closer than they would otherwise. Personally, I don't shy away from using university-level or A Level standard writing as a model for my secondary school pupils; I simply scaffold or explain any elements that are more challenging to understand. When writing models as well as you can, you'll often hit the criteria for a top band answer, without worrying inordinately about exemplifying a particular grade. You'll also then be modelling what great academic writing looks like and avoiding some of the pitfalls associated with grade-focused feedback. If students then try to write to the same level, they will automatically be closer to achieving highly, without needing to continually focus on grades.

You can use this strategy even for lower or mixed attainment sets to avoid placing limitations on their achievement. You can support them to understand a written response through scaffolding and, in so doing, will help them to develop much more sophisticated answers than if you simply gave them a 'Grade 5' model. More importantly, students won't become obsessed with grades and marks at the expense of developing a genuine interest in the subject. You will, of course, want to consult the exam specification to inform your planning and to ensure your examples contains key elements, but you do not necessarily need to aim for a grade-linked piece. For example, we can talk about what makes a thoughtful comparison of sources, what elements a fantastic translation will contain, or the ingredients of an incredibly persuasive speech, for instance. I accept that this approach may be more difficult in a subject such as maths with its often 'right or wrong' answers than an essay-based subject, but teachers might harness some of its benefits by referencing how a particular skill or element of the curriculum enables learning or achievement at high levels in 'real life' as well as simply the achievement of a grade. This could be done by referencing the application of trigonometry to engineering, for instance, or highlighting how a particular concept lays the foundation for future learning.

If you do teach an essay-based subject, you might go about writing model answers in this way:

- Write a model answer based simply on what you are able to write, to the best of *your* ability, in a response to an exam question for your class.
- Then go back and look at the response: what are the best parts of the answer? Reflect on how you can explain to your class *why* these parts are so effective.
- If you are preparing for an assessment, you can check whether the 'best bits' correspond with the exam mark scheme and make any adjustments you deem necessary, but you do not always need to explicitly share this with students – especially at an early point in the unit.
- Reflect on whether any elements of the model answer need scaffolding. You might provide definitions of vocabulary you have used, explanations of your writing style, or share the response section by section in detail, rather than as one piece.
- Remember that the level of the content does not need to directly fit the level of output we expect from a group. If we write a 'Year 7 model answer' we arguably place limits on children and a ceiling on their aspirations. If we write something at a much higher level and scaffold this appropriately, we give them something exciting and aspirational to work towards and can inspire students with the resources we use.

The problem with the ZPD

When I have shared this approach and philosophy with other teachers, I have occasionally been asked whether it might not be damaging to our lower attaining pupils to be confronted with examples or model answers that are, at their current level of study, unrealistic for them to achieve. Detractors might argue that giving students high-level responses is problematic in light of the concept that we learn based on existing schemata and that students need to work within their Zone of Proximal Development (ZPD) in order to make progress. The prevailing concept of the ZPD – or, the idea of teaching students at a level just beyond their current stage – has pervaded education to such an extent that to introduce anything in a lesson at a level significantly beyond students' current ability seems counterintuitive. However, Smagorinsky (2018) argues that the concept of the ZPD has been over-simplified and misapplied to the extent that it is often simply understood as referring to instructional scaffolding in the immediate space of the classroom, when in fact, the ZPD is better understood as referring to a long-term developmental process. He points out that whilst Vygotsky used metaphorical language to suggest that the 'buds' and 'flowers' of development that exist today will emerge as 'fruits' of learning 'tomorrow' (Vygotsky, 1978:86-87), the concept of 'tomorrow' has been interpreted by many English speakers too literally. In fact, Vygotsky probably meant 'tomorrow' to be understood metaphorically as 'the future' rather than in the literal sense of the next day or as the direct next stage of learning.

By pitching all learning in a manner directly linked to what we believe students can do now and what is only *just* beyond their capabilities, we may not stretch them far enough. I would argue it may not sow enough seeds or harness enough buds to eventually flower into the fruits of long-term learning. By misinterpreting or even over-relying on the concept of the ZPD, we can occasionally verge on being too worried about only introducing students to concepts or levels of work that lie just beyond their current capability. Not every aspect of every lesson needs to be aimed 'just above' students' current level – our conception of the ZPD should be more nuanced than that.

The concept of 'pitching' a lesson to the right level and the next stage in students' development is important in teaching in order not to overwhelm our learners and to harness schematic knowledge. However, pitching *may* – when taken too literally – lead some teachers to shy away from incorporating their most advanced knowledge of their subject, as we aim for the next grade or level. Similarly, the concept of 'teaching to the top' has been used to mean pitching lesson content at a level just above current learning: for example, a 'Grade 7' level, if most of the class are working at Grades 5, 6 and 7. However, there is something of a logical sticking point here. Firstly, it isn't how life works – it is only how learning works in certain circumstances. While the notion of pitching learning in the ZPD is invaluable when it comes to scaffolding *tasks,* assessments and what students do, it is less helpful when it comes to framing the *examples* students are shown to inspire, motivate or shape their conception of achievement in the subject. If we look around at society and other examples of education and learning beyond the school classroom, we can see that we do not only look to those people working 'just above' our own level in order to achieve.

High-level examples and practising perfect form

A good example of 'learning from the top' whilst working in your ZPD can probably be found in your local gym. I enjoy lifting weights in my spare time. I know very well that I am nowhere near as good or as strong as a professional weightlifter, and unlikely ever to be. But anyone doing any type of weightlifting should look at examples of excellent form and use these to help them improve. Every move must be done with perfect form – even if you are lifting relatively light weights – otherwise, the consequence can be either injury or embedding bad habits that are hard to break as your strength increases. Watching other weightlifters lifting much heavier weights doesn't make me feel inadequate at all. I know I am not the best in the gym or the most successful but I keep trying because I can see myself improving and I can use others as examples to strive towards.

I look both to people who are amazing to help me see what the goal is, and then I also look at people in the gym who are slightly better than me to help me see the next step. It sounds overly simplistic, but my point is that we can balance our notion of the ZPD and grade-focused feedback by giving students incredible examples from scholarship to aspire to. We have over-complicated what it means to make progress and reduced opportunities for high-level learning by always focusing on 'the grade above' or the 'next step' in the ZPD. By teaching to the very top and not worrying too much about grades, we ironically empower our pupils to later reach these lofty heights eventually. We also avoid embedding a sense of failure for those who aren't there yet.

Similarly, when we are at university, we tend to read journal articles by academics rather than other undergraduates. Encountering these examples of high-quality research helps us to become better thinkers, researchers and writers. While the majority of us don't attain the same standard of writing during our undergraduate degree, encountering such a high level of writing helps us get pretty close. When learning to be a better swimmer, we can use techniques also used by top athletes in order to swim faster and better. We won't necessarily be the next Michael Phelps or Rebecca Adlington, but using some of the strategies can help us to get quicker and stronger. When we watch cookery programmes, we want to see great cookery so that we can attempt some approximation of this ourselves in the kitchen. I could go on because the same goes for almost any other sport, activity or pursuit.

We also might think about how young children learn to talk. We don't teach them how to speak by only using words they already know and then occasionally adding a new word into the mix. That would be absurd. We might avoid using the word 'antidisestablishmentarianism', and use simpler, repetitive expressions or 'baby talk' to scaffold the child's use of language. However, we automatically use a far broader vocabulary than the child can use, and intuitively help them to develop their language with techniques such as repetition and explaining or showing them what particular words mean. The result, of course, is that their vocabulary development is far more rapid than it would be if we were to limit our language to a pre-set selection of words pitched just above the child's current level. And yet, when it comes to academic study in school, we sometimes shy away from teaching students key concepts or ideas for fear that it might be too far beyond their 'current level' or 'target grade'. It seems logical, but we need to be exposed to the best to ever hope to reach the top. If we only ever show students aiming for a Grade 6 examples or models of 'what a Grade 6 looks like', they are far less likely to ever achieve that grade than if we had exposed them to higher-level examples. It is likely to be far more effective to pitch our teaching much higher than the grade 'just above' the students' current level; to aim teaching to the top of our knowledge level, scaffolding students' understanding and our explanations to help them formulate their understanding of a high-quality response.

Balance and framing

So, to apply this in the classroom, we should show students amazing examples of scholarship but should avoid linking this to grades, because if we do then students are likely to see and judge the gap between their own ability and the grades at the top in a self-critical or negative way. When setting goals, we can have overarching goals of becoming a better mathematician, fantastic academic writer, impressive French speaker, or insightful historian, and so on, rather than simply getting a certain mark. When we need to make goals more specific, we can focus on one or two elements, but this does not necessarily need to be based on marks or grades.

Furthermore, to preserve the confidence and self-esteem of learners of all levels, the key to teaching to the top rather than the test when it comes to modelling is in both the *balance* and the *framing*. By balance, I mean that we can provide examples from other learners' work and other responses close to students' current level, alongside examples from higher-level study. Peer-to-peer learning is valuable, especially when students can see how others have incorporated elements of top-level examples in their own work. For example, in English, we might show students the work of a professional writer alongside sharing on the visualiser where their peers have incorporated elements of successful writing in their own work. In terms of balance, it is also the case that to some extent, what you see or introduce to students as 'the top' may differ depending on the age or attainment level of the class. But to achieve the goal of 'aiming above the mark' that I refer to here, the examples given need to be significantly beyond students' target grades and they need to be inspirational. Secondly, by framing, I mean to say that the language we use around high-level examples when 'teaching to the top' helps avoid any issues associated with students feeling inferior or insecure in comparison. We can watch an Olympic athlete or see the work of a world-class artist without feeling insecure about our own skills as we are aware we are watching someone at the top of their game. Likewise, when we frame examples of great work in our subject for students, we can describe it as an incredible example that we do not expect students to reach or attain yet. We can frame it as a possible and attainable goal to achieve one day, but not something that we necessarily expect students to do in a day, week or month. Students need to believe both that we do not expect them to reach this standard easily or quickly, but also that they are capable of striving for the top one day.

To embed this most effectively, we can teach to the very top in terms of examples, knowledge shared and content, but scaffold and pitch more carefully when it comes to student work. In some circumstances, we have conflated tasks and examples. While the use of a visualiser to share student work can be a fantastic AFL and feedback strategy for classes, seeing examples of high-quality Year 7 responses might be more useful for other Year 7s to see at key points during the process of writing their own responses. Before they write, we can show them something significantly above Year 7 level to challenge them conceptually, model excellence and introduce them to ideas beyond their current level. Similarly, GCSE students can, for example, be taught A Level standard ideas, academic phrasing or critical concepts, whilst still being scaffolded and supported to answer examination questions. A Level students can be shown examples that wouldn't be out of place in a third-year university exam, and so on. Some might argue that continually being shown high-level examples can be damaging to students' motivation when they are working far below that level. I would counter that it is more harmful for students to compare themselves against a 'Grade 9' or the highest achieving student in the class. (For more detail on why within-class comparisons can be damaging, see the research I explore on academic self-concept in Chapter 8.) An example from scholarship, or from beyond a Year 11 level, can be framed as an inspirational goal to include elements of, rather than as a certain grade. Using these strategies, I have repeatedly helped students to achieve grades far above those predicted for them.

A caveat here is that with some subjects, such as mathematics – which can often require the mastering of a base concept or skill before being capable of moving on – the idea of always carefully pitching learning *just* above the current level of understanding makes more sense. I am by no means suggesting that the concept of pitch is useless or unhelpful. I am, though, suggesting that perhaps we may have allowed it to pervade learning too deeply, in light of our data-obsessed school system. When it comes to subjects such as the humanities, English, languages, or the sciences, it is easy to think of examples of times when teaching ideas far beyond the students' current knowledge level can be hugely beneficial, inspiring and motivating.

QUESTIONS FOR REFLECTION

- In which elements of your subject could you use high-level examples from scholarship or from 'real life' rather than graded examples?
- Think about your university-level knowledge. Are there any advanced concepts you might introduce, with scaffolded explanations, to lower year groups?
- Remember that *tasks* should be pitched at the right level (although they should facilitate an element of challenge) but *examples* can be inspiring and can far exceed students' current level. Where in your current curriculum plans could you use higher-level models? Can you afford to dedicate more time to their deconstruction and analysis?
- Are there any points where your curriculum or certain topics you teach may rely too much on the concept of working *just above* a current level? Are there any times that higher-level concepts could be interwoven into lessons?
- Are there any areas of your curriculum plan where grade-based feedback can be replaced with a formative option?
- In what ways are the concepts of balance and framing relevant to the curriculum in your subject?

Chapter 5

The dangers of differentiation

'We're all in the gutter, but some of us are looking at the stars.' – Oscar Wilde

Differentiation by expectation: why it prevents us from teaching to the top

On my first day of teaching as an enthusiastic and nervous newly qualified teacher, I walked into my new classroom and felt my heart sink at the sight of three enormous laminated posters tacked to the whiteboard. One red, one orange, and one green. In capital letters on each poster were the words: All. Most. Some. Those three words filled me with dread as I thought about the message they would transmit to any child entering my classroom. Even as a new teacher, I knew those words didn't communicate ambition and aspiration. They suggested that some children would be expected to achieve the very best in my classes and the rest would not. A few would meet my most challenging objectives, but most wouldn't. I knew that it wasn't a message I could tolerate being stuck on the board behind me. As a new member of staff, I was loath to offend whoever had last had that classroom, and I wasn't sure who the room had belonged to before me or whether they still worked at the school. Nonetheless, I was desperate to tear those posters down. How long had they been there? What if it had been my mentor or my head of department who had put them up and they quizzed me about where they had gone? My nerves as a new teacher did make me hesitate but the feeling of unease grew stronger than my worry about offending anyone else. By the end of my first day, I had shoved the posters in the bottom of a drawer where they languished for the remainder of the year. (At that stage of my career, I wasn't quite brave enough to throw them in the bin!) I was never asked about the posters, but the reason for their existence soon became clear when I saw the school's official observation forms which required me to set 'all', 'most' and 'some' objectives for lessons. Again, I quietly ignored the requirement to use these objectives and only incorporated them into my lessons when I was being officially observed.

So why was my reaction so strong? I wasn't usually particularly outspoken as a new teacher and certainly didn't make a habit of ignoring directives from SLT. If anything, I was desperately keen to please and impress in the job I had been so excited to begin. The reason, in this case, was simple – I knew I couldn't ask children to put themselves in boxes according to their preconceived ability. I knew my ambitions would be the same for every child. Whether or not this might sound rather idealistic, it is a belief that comes from a place of passion for the ability of every child to succeed and a desire not to place limitations on anyone who sits in front of me in my classroom. When we teach, our own vision of education inevitably informs our approach and I wouldn't have become a teacher in the first place if I thought I was going to place limits on the aspirations of any child in my classroom. That is not to say that I thought every child in my class would achieve the highest grades, but I didn't want any of them to think that they *couldn't*. I wanted them to know that I would provide each of them with access to the highest levels of knowledge and understanding that I could. So, dividing the class into 'all', 'most' and 'some' boxes didn't cohere with that philosophy.

I'm sure I made countless mistakes over the course of that first year – which NQT hasn't? But one thing I never regretted was taking those posters down. It's a way of thinking that has stayed with me. If we stand in front of our classes and tell our children that they belong to different categories of achievement, that they all have different targets and should be working 'at' different levels, we entrench the idea of preconceived ability. Even if these differentiated objectives are labelled 'must, should, could', 'bronze, silver, gold', or 'Grade 7, 8, 9', they prevent us from teaching to the top for *everyone*. Perhaps even worse is the use of teacher-set targets during a lesson, where a teacher might tell students, 'If your target is a Grade 5 you should do the first activity, but if it's a 6, your task is the second one.' If we base our aspirations for children on their prior attainment, then we inevitably restrict what our students perceive themselves as capable of doing.

Differentiation by support makes sense, but differentiation by expectation, setting and curriculum planning is not evidence-informed and can further entrench the attainment gap. The Pygmalion effect discussed previously in this book (Rosenthal, 1968) tells us that the higher our expectations of students, the more likely they are to achieve well. More contemporary research has demonstrated that even implicit differences in teachers' expectations of students' abilities are inferred by students and can affect their achievement (Rubie-Davies, 2006), so it stands to reason that when these different expectations are explicitly shared, the negative impact on some students in a classroom will inevitably be even worse. And if the notion of ability as fixed is emphasised to students, or the idea that they are in a certain 'category' within the class, it also seems likely that this could prevent our students from developing a 'growth mindset' (Dweck, 2008) in which they see targets as motivation to improve. Think about which children are likely to put themselves in the 'all' category. Imagine which of your students would be likely to aim lower than they need to, if they have not got the level of self-esteem and prior achievement that has enabled them to develop a conception of themselves as one of the select few in the 'some' category. How might students' internalized self-perception affect how they see themselves and where they, as a result, aim to get? Even more significantly, our unconscious or implicit bias as teachers might be likely to influence where we tell students they should be aiming; research evidence demonstrates that we all unconsciously form stereotypical associations and make inaccurate judgements about people (Greenwald and Krieger, 2006).

We shouldn't blame teachers or school leaders for the misguided approach of using differentiated learning objectives or target-driven outcomes. Only a few years ago, it was commonplace for Ofsted to check whether students were aware of their target grades and their 'working at' level or to criticise teachers for not differentiating by task. Differentiated learning objectives would hardly have become as popular as they were without external pressures on schools, but it is a form of differentiation that limits, rather than enables, our young people. Instead of differentiating by task or by objective, the differentiation necessary in a classroom where we teach to the top is supportive. For instance, differentiation might involve provision of sentence starters or writing frames, vocabulary, dual coding or different forms of explanations. Methods such as these are immensely preferable to separating students into groups in which we expect less of some students before we have even given them a chance to try the activity. However, the dangerous, harmful impact of differentiation does not begin in the classroom with differentiated learning objectives or differing expectations for some children. In many schools, it begins with the setting system.

Differentiation by setting: placing limits on learning

Grouping students into sets isn't often viewed as differentiation but, of course, it is. It is one of the most significant forms of differentiation that schools have at their disposal as it entails splitting students into 'ability' groups which determine their entire experience of education. You will notice in this chapter that I largely avoid using the terms 'higher/ lower ability' – unless enclosed in inverted commas – believing as I do that ability is not a fixed entity. I prefer 'higher and lower attaining' to explicitly emphasise this distinction, as the term recognises the malleable nature of ability. Yet the nature of setting means that some students will be differentiated into the bottom or lowest sets and classified as 'lower ability' when they have barely had a chance to begin their learning in a subject. In some schools, this might be at the beginning of Year 7 and based heavily on SATs results from primary school or tests taken on a student's entry to the school. In some schools, setting happens in almost every subject, whilst in others it is only in core subjects, but the practice, to some degree, is nearly ubiquitous in UK secondary schools. This is in spite of the fact that setting has, overall, a detrimental effect on student achievement; research has repeatedly failed to find that it has any significant benefits (Francis et al, 2016). Further to this, Taylor et al (2016) found that schools set in spite of extensive evidence which suggests it is detrimental to the majority of pupils' achievement, due to factors including concerns that mixed-ability classes are viewed as unconventional and are disliked by parents. International comparisons indicate that student achievement is higher in more equal societies in which students are taught in mixed attainment groups (Wilkinson and Pickett, 2009), and a meta-analysis by the Education Endowment

Foundation (2021) also indicates that setting and streaming have a detrimental impact on student progress and that disadvantaged pupils, in particular, tend to make less progress in streamed ability groups. I would posit that this may be partly because disadvantaged pupils are more likely, for a range of reasons – including societal bias – to be placed in lower sets and therefore less likely, in the current system of schooling, to have access to teachers who are teaching to the top. They are also more likely, due to contextual factors, to underachieve in their SATs and therefore to be placed in lower sets by schools that stream on Year 7 entry.

And yet, despite the panoply of problems associated with it, setting continues, accepted as an unproblematic status quo in the majority of secondary schools. It is ironic that many schools that have implemented research-informed pedagogies and have abandoned pseudoscientific practices (such as 'learning styles' or 'brain gym) continue to implement setting with seemingly little reflection on its impact. Jackson (2010) and Taylor et al (2016) found that mixed attainment teaching has been a source of fear for teachers and schools concerned about changes to their practice. While some school leaders might be unaware of the research on setting, it seems likely that, in some cases, even though we know that setting isn't effective, it persists largely because we aren't brave enough to do away with it.

Let's pause for a moment to think about the students who come to us in Year 7 only to be swiftly placed in a 'bottom set' or on a particular 'flight path' with a low target grade. Before reaching secondary school, many of the students who will be placed in the bottom set have probably been placed on the bottom 'table' or lowest attaining within-class group in their primary school class. Once they make it into Year 7, not only are these students once again placed in a bottom group due to data but they are also assigned a target that, in many schools, is drawn from data partly based on their prior attainment, such as SATs scores. This is likely to stay the same for the next five years and determine the grade students are expected to achieve in their GCSEs. While the removal of the requirement for Ofsted to examine a school's internal data (Department for Education, 2019) means that some schools are now less likely to regularly give students feedback based on whether they are meeting their target grades, others have merely adapted the feedback system to be less focused on grades and to report to students whether they are 'below', 'meeting' or 'exceeding' expected progress. The trouble here, though, is that every child's progress, expectations and targets are still continually linked to their prior achievement, with less expected of students who have previously achieved less highly. Rather than doing all we can to level the playing field, we place lower prior attaining students in groups where their achievement will most likely be even more limited. This means that schools become – rather than meritocracies – deterministic environments in which it is difficult for students to escape from the grade-labelled boxes they have been placed inside.

It is only the fact that these systems have long existed in schools that makes us accept them unquestioningly. If we were introducing them in the present day it would be obvious that they are entirely counterproductive for an education system that purports to strive for social justice. Even teachers marking students' work in bottom sets may be influenced, due to unconscious bias or prior teaching, to expect less from that student and therefore to mark them more harshly. Furthermore, the child may be denied access to the high-level ideas that are explored in top sets, not only due to their target grades and teachers' conceptions of their 'ability', but also due to not being taught alongside high-attaining students who might ask challenging questions or use more sophisticated vocabulary. Proponents of setting would argue that even in a bottom set, a teacher can still stretch and challenge pupils and incorporate high-level ideas, and indeed they can, as I explore later in this chapter. Yet whilst we can do our best to mitigate the harm of a damaging structure, the existence of ability grouping nevertheless systematically limits the achievement of some. Sets have been shown to harm students' self-esteem (Ireson and Hallam, 2001) and limit their academic achievement, plausibly by denying students access to the highest-level ideas and creating a self-fulfilling prophecy of low achievement.

Setting systems are accepted as an integral part of the education system in many schools and yet act in direct opposition to social justice. The same schools which emphasise the importance of education for all and 'closing the gap' between students who receive free school meals and those who do not frequently see no issue with the fact that, in a setting system, poorer students are more likely to be in the bottom group due to a raft of socioeconomic factors impacting their achievement. We have a wealth of research demonstrating the statistical underachievement of certain demographics such as Black Caribbean children (Demie and McLean, 2017) and white working-class boys (Kirby and Cullinane, 2016), and yet we also work within a system that often, based on the results these children obtain in tests incredibly early in their school life, places them in groups where work will be pitched at a lower level, where expectations are limited, and a ceiling is placed on achievement.

Differentiating for pupils at the top: surely we are meant to 'stretch and challenge' our highest prior attainers?

While setting has been demonstrated to have a negative impact on pupils, research suggests that there can be positive benefits for students in the highest groups (Ireson and Hallam, 2001). If students are in the top set, ability groupings *might* have a positive effect on achievement according to Hattie's review of effect sizes (2009:99). This stands to reason, as being around others who are working at a higher level and motivated by the higher expectations of a teacher who expects the best is bound to have a positive impact on students. However, can the detrimental impact of setting on student self-esteem, self-belief and achievement across the cohort really be justified simply due to the prioritisation of a select few? Is that really the kind of value system we should be emphasising as teachers? Should we be stating, implicitly, that the highest attaining students matter but others do not? It shows something extremely troubling about what we value as educators if we choose to prioritise the attainment of a handful of high achievers over the success of the majority.

The previous Ofsted inspection handbook made reference to schools making provision of the 'most able' alongside pupils with special educational needs but made no special mention of pupils in the middle. Likewise, the previous Department for Education used the term 'gifted and talented' and many schools still have a 'Gifted and Talented Coordinator' or a similar role for a member of staff responsible for pushing the 'most able' to achieve. This is often accepted unquestioningly, but how can it be right to label a few students as the brightest at an early stage and then direct interventions specifically at those students who, in many cases, are already achieving well? If some pupils are given the label of 'G&T', 'most able', 'high attaining' or however we define it, that means that, as a result, many others are not. The gifted and talented pupils might be offered a trip to Cambridge University in Year 8, additional academic experiences, or opportunities to engage with external providers in opportunities to stretch them intellectually. That's fantastic for those children but what about those who are not given the chance? What happens to those who had a bad day on their SATs day or entry tests? What happens to those who have already had a lifetime of poverty and disadvantage and now have to miss out on yet another academic opportunity?

Being labelled as 'high prior attaining' or 'Gifted and Talented' can have an immensely positive impact on a select few, but for others who don't 'make the grade', they miss out on this. In my own childhood, I was one of the lucky ones. One day when I was in Year 7 my deputy headteacher came to tell me I was on the Gifted and Talented 'register', which erroneously evoked in my eleven-year-old mind the image of a weighty tome of names added to over the years to which I had been, along with a select few, granted admittance. I went from someone who was rather underconfident at the start of Year 7 to someone with a newfound sense of confidence in my own abilities. Before long, I was completing extra homework during the holidays and writing endless poems to share with my beleaguered English teacher. I was wandering around my house practising my French out loud and my overzealous hand shot into the air so often during history and science class that I'm very lucky I had any friends at all. How lucky for me; how very fortunate I was. I hadn't sat the SATs, so simply due to doing well in the Year 7 entry tests, I was set for success in secondary school. I thought I could achieve, and so I was bound to. I was also lucky enough to have a supportive family and I did enjoy learning at primary school, but I can trace a lot of my absolute determination to do well – and my belief that I should be aiming high – to that conversation. I learned that I was an A* student, so I became one.

Unfortunately, some students learn the exact opposite, so the reverse happens to them. How utterly unfair is that? When we put children in top sets or create special groups and workshops for high prior attaining pupils, we take those students who are already ahead and we give them even more confidence to believe they can achieve anything. This would be brilliant if it wasn't for all the other children who are *not* afforded the same boost in confidence and self-belief. Those who have it reinforced to them at an early stage that they are 'average' or 'lower ability'. Those who are put in a different sort of academic box to the very cosy one I was put into. The boost in confidence and exciting opportunities given to a select few is arguably not worth the cost to the rest of the student body. Instead, we should be showing belief in the potential of all our students and providing opportunities for all of them to be intellectually challenged.

The 'values cost' of ability grouping

Hattie (2009:255) notes that even when research suggests an intervention might have a positive effect in some circumstances, we must consider the costs as well as the benefits of innovations. While Hattie was speaking generally here and was not referring to ability grouping or special treatment for high prior attaining students, this cost can be interpreted in a broader sense than merely as budgetary or in terms of time taken by an intervention. We also might consider, I think, the emotional cost or the 'values cost' for our schools if we emphasise difference rather than shared goals and shared access to the same education. We must critically reflect on the cost for *other* pupils if we direct some interventions only at a select few students identified as 'gifted' or 'high prior attaining'. While it might be wonderful for those select pupils, what is lost in terms of other children's future motivation and self-belief? We need to put ourselves in the position of those children for whom failure is embedded in their timetable when they see a string of Band Ds or Set 5s at the beginning of September and seriously reflect on whether we can justify this in light of the cost.

If you're still not convinced, think back for a moment to your first day of university. Remember your first day? That exciting moment of walking into your first lecture. Can you imagine being made to take a test on that first day and, depending on the result, being placed in one of five groups?

And then imagine being placed in the bottom group. Imagine how it would feel. What would have been the resulting impact on your drive, enthusiasm and motivation for your studies? How would it have affected your self-perception and self-belief? Whether you eventually came out at the end with a First or a Third, would it have been right for you to feel you were predestined to be in the Third or First group from the start, according to a set group? Or let's say you attend a watercolour class in your spare time. On your first day, you know you aren't the most skilled artist in the class but you are motivated to improve. However, the second time you attend the class, it is split into several groups and you are placed in the bottom one. Even worse, you're assigned a different teacher than the one you had originally and this teacher doesn't let you try out the more sophisticated techniques you know that the top group is learning about. You know that you might struggle with the more advanced methods, but you'd like to have a go anyway. The teacher says you can't. That's for the top set and *you* have to focus on the basics first. Such an approach would hardly improve your engagement with the class. You might not even go back. When we imagine setting in other contexts other than the one we have become inured to, simply due to the fact that it is 'how it's always been done', the issues with it become glaring.

It is true that in many schools, teachers try to mitigate the damage of setting systems by allowing pupils to move between sets depending on their current progress, but their motivation to work hard enough to move up is likely to be interrelated with their self-esteem as extensive research suggests that pupils' self-confidence can be negatively affected by the setting system (Francis et al, 2020). Thinking from a pragmatic perspective, how could it not be? If students are told that they are in the lowest-achieving group, this is hardly going to inspire and motivate them. I am not suggesting that students with special educational needs do not sometimes need special treatment in some ways – of course, they might sometimes need additional support, scaffolding and help to access the curriculum. I am also not suggesting that there are *no* circumstances in which attainment grouping *may* be helpful, but the research does suggest that the circumstances in which setting is beneficial are ultimately very few and far between. For example, many of us currently teach in schools where students with dyslexia or who speak English as an additional language may automatically end up in bottom sets due to their performance on reading and writing tests. Subsequently, students who are cognitively able to access the curriculum nevertheless are taught in classes where they are less likely to be exposed to high-level vocabulary and knowledge. There is a fundamental moral problem here that we arguably do not spend enough time reflecting on as teachers and leaders.

In subjects that do not have tiered examinations, 'more able' students are taught in a different way to 'less able' students and then are expected to sit the same examination at the end of the course, having been pre-limited by their sets. It is important to note that, in many schools, fantastic teachers do a wonderful job of teaching to the top even within the bottom set, but the very existence of sets in the first place puts an external limit on children's self-perception and achievement that we then have to fight against. Many teachers who have taught bottom sets are likely to have stories about the low self-perception of students. Last year, I taught a Year 8 bottom set who found out that I was doing a PhD. After I explained what this was, one of them asked me: 'Miss, but you're really clever. Why are you teaching the bottom set?' Even one of the children in the class had a pre-conceived idea that as a lower attaining child, he would not be entitled to a knowledgeable teacher. It is this deep lack of self-esteem that the setting system contributes to creating. Ultimately, whilst teachers in so many schools try to mitigate the damage of setting by teaching well regardless of the set they teach, they are having to do this within a system that is fundamentally flawed and not evidence-informed.

Teaching to the top in a system that pushes some to the bottom

Even though sets work to perpetuate disadvantage and social injustice, the reality is that most of us at secondary level are still forced to teach in a system in which they are imposed upon us. So how can you still work to mitigate the negative consequences wrought by setting, particularly if you are given the bottom set by the 'powers that be' within your school? Quite simply, by teaching to the top as far as possible, in every single lesson you teach.

If you teach a bottom or a lower set, you can help to work against the disadvantages and problems of setting by adjusting lesson content as little as possible between your top and bottom set classes. This would be a controversial statement in some schools where you are expected to show how you have differentiated your materials for each class and it may even be seen as a mark of laziness to take the same lesson material and deliver it to Set 1 and then Set 4. In fact, it is an act of high aspirations and an envisioning of social justice to provide the same quality of education for each class. Of course, some may need help to access the materials – writing frames, scaffolds in the form of keyword definitions or pre-teaching of vocabulary, to name a few examples. However, the level of high-quality knowledge to which we expose students and the core curriculum content must be the same or as similar as possible to avoid widening the attainment gap still further. As teachers working with bottom sets, we should strike a fine balance between exposing students to a high level of knowledge but also supporting them to access this knowledge and to achieve. We can also work to point out what students are good at and make it our mission to boost their confidence whenever we can. In Chapter 4, I wrote about the importance of balance and framing when teaching to the top and the same strategy applies when teaching any class including bottom sets. We can frame the challenge of high-level examples as exciting and inspiring rather than intimidating, and we can balance the sharing of top-level academic knowledge with also giving examples of students' work at a stage closer to our own pupils' level.

You can expect some resistance in your lower sets when teaching to the top. You can expect disillusionment to creep in at first but don't *accept* these things. Challenge it at every turn. Don't let low expectations or low targets be an option. Boost their self-esteem by giving them the tools to reach a high level through scaffolding. (See Chapter 8 for more details on how to give children the confidence to succeed when teaching to the top.) Believe that they can achieve highly and understand complex concepts – always remember that teachers' expectations shape students' abilities to achieve. To that end, try not to talk negatively even with colleagues about teaching 'Set 5' or whatever the equivalent is in your school. If you work to bring a positive, high-aspiration mindset to the lessons, students will be much more likely to achieve highly. Some of my best relationships with classes, and some of my students' most impressive examination results, have come from those pupils who initially resisted the high expectations I set for them.

Also – since we know that setting and ability streaming are not evidence-informed and are detrimental to progress and self-esteem – if you are forced to teach in a setting system, don't overstate the value of that system to your students. For example, avoid telling them, 'if you work hard on this test you might go up a set' or similar. Instead, work to show them that sets aren't particularly meaningful or important; the important thing is how they progress as an individual. Within my lower sets, I regularly de-emphasise the importance of setting and ability grouping. For instance, I tell my students that their target grades are just a piece of paper and are essentially meaningless compared to the grades they will walk out with. I tell them that no one, as soon as they have left school, will ever ask what set they were in. They will, however, want to know what they learned in school and, depending on their career ambitions, what their exam results were.

Fundamentally, when teaching a class of any attainment level, we need to remember to use our high-level subject knowledge and embed it in planning. Every child should be given access to the highest-level knowledge and does not deserve their pre-existing data to place limitations on what they can achieve. Teaching to the top for a lower attaining class may require more scaffolding but it is vital if we are to ensure all students, including those more likely statistically to be from disadvantaged backgrounds, to be afforded a rich and challenging education. If we are forced to teach in sets, the least we can do is try to shed the 'bottom set mindset' as teachers and help learners to do the same. By teaching to the top, no matter the class, we can help our students to mentally break free from the ability boxes that the school system has placed them in.

QUESTIONS FOR REFLECTION

- In your own classroom, what strategies do you use to show that 'ability' is not fixed? Are there any ways you could further work to instil that belief in students?
- How does setting affect students in your school specifically?
- Are there any topics within which you differentiate by task? How could this be replaced by teaching to the top and scaffolding and support as differentiation?
- If you are a leader, is there any scope to reduce the use of 'ability' grouping or attainment-based setting in your school, given the extensive research that suggests it is detrimental?
- Do teachers and leaders in your school still talk about the 'high prior attaining' or 'G&T' students? If so, what strategies could you use in your setting to bring about a mindset shift to teaching to the top for all?

Chapter 6

Teaching to the top with flexibility, adaptability and spontaneity

'When it is obvious that the goals cannot be reached, don't adjust the goals, adjust the action steps.' – Confucius

The problem with set lesson structures

The current Ofsted inspection framework does not recommend any one type of lesson structure, apart from stating that teachers should explain subject content clearly, promote discussion, check for understanding and provide clear feedback in lessons. However, it is commonplace in a number of schools and academy trusts for leaders to implement set lesson structures they expect teachers to use, such as using particular three, four or five-part lesson plans containing certain elements. These elements might include research-informed parts, such as a retrieval practice starter, direct instruction, independent writing and a plenary. The reasoning for this is understandable, as the use of each of these practices is supported by research and valuable in a range of circumstances. Yet when we mandate a rigid formula that a lesson must follow or a checklist of things it must unequivocally contain, we oversimplify educational research to the extent that we lose our ability to be critically reflective in our own classrooms.

No matter how efficacious a pedagogical method is in many circumstances, or how supported by evidence in some contexts, it is not the case that any method can be applied wholesale to every lesson and assumed to be the best in every situation. Professor Dylan Wiliam put this best in 2019 when he argued that teachers need to be 'critical consumers of research' who recognise that the validity of a particular approach or piece of research depends heavily on their individual context. Teaching cannot be *based* on research but only informed by it, due to the innumerable ways in which the context, aims and practice of a lesson may vary. It is tempting to think that if 'the research says' then a pedagogical technique is effective and must work well in every scenario. Whenever we make anything universal and obligatory, we restrict the possibility for alternative approaches to be utilised which also might be research-informed, useful and productive in the right circumstances.

Conceivably, we may also detract from deep learning by using a set lesson structure by preventing learning that veers from a pre-determined path, or limiting any possibility for flexibility as the teacher responds to students' learning within the lesson itself. John (2006) suggests that the embedding of set expectations for lesson structures in teacher training courses and schools can lead to a restricted approach to teaching and learning. Lesson planning should, instead, be emphasised as context-dependent, to enable beginning teachers to develop reflective engagement with the learning process and to be able to justify specific planning decisions with reference to the subject and topic being taught. Further to this, when we focus on the outcome of just one particular lesson, we may concentrate too much on the assessment at the expense of other learning possibilities. Reductive lesson planning structures and set pedagogies of instruction which allow for little deviation from a particular format could move us away from a process of reflective engagement and be detrimental to teaching and learning.

Similarly, David Didau made the point in 2015 on his blog *The Learning Spy* that by focusing our attention too much on individual lessons, we may focus too much on what students *do* in terms of activity rather than what they are learning over time. He suggests that whilst lessons are the way the curriculum must be delivered, they do not need to be the vehicle for planning. Formulaic planning structures can also prevent teachers from drawing on the full extent of their expertise and subject knowledge and can prevent reflective teaching (Bage et al, 1999). They do not work for teaching to the top because they can inhibit our ability to judge where depth of thought is needed. For instance, in many cases, rushing to fit in several elements within one lesson can be detrimental to learning by preventing us from spending extended periods on developing key concepts or ideas. Sometimes it may make sense, therefore, for learning to be planned over the course of a week or several lessons, with the route taken to get to our objective made more flexible. Set lesson types also harm teachers as well as restricting the joy, variety and flexibility of learning. A large-scale quantitative study commissioned by the National Foundation for Educational Research found that mandated lesson structures risk increasing retention difficulties due to loss of morale and job satisfaction (Worth and Van den Brande, 2020).

The value of flexibility

When we move away from the notion of a set multi-part lesson, we make space for flexibility and for deep learning that does not need to fit within a pre-determined box or number of minutes. For instance, in English, it might occasionally be appropriate to spend most of the lesson reading a book before moving on to analysis at a later date in a process of 'cold reading' (Webb, 2019). Or it might be appropriate to have an extended discussion exploring deeper meanings and concepts relating to a source text, or on listening to the delivery of students' presentations which they have carefully prepared over the preceding weeks. In history, a teacher may wish to spend a whole lesson analysing a source with their class and discussing it in depth before writing about it in the next lesson. Or perhaps it is fitting to devote a whole lesson to facilitating a critical debate or to extended research. In French, students might need an hour to complete a challenging translation task they have built up to throughout a unit, or taking part in a speaking and listening carousel. In one lesson, it could make sense to have ten quick-fire activities to suit the learning objective, while in another, it would be better to focus on just one activity, to allow students to apply their prior learning.

Occasionally, it might not be appropriate to begin a lesson with retrieval practice. Instead, it could be preferable to engage students with a 'big question' that the lesson content hinges on. As I explore in the next chapter, instead of direct instruction, it might be productive to draw out the learning aims through dialogic learning or Socratic questioning. In creative subjects, dedicating a whole lesson to one activity could also enable students to fully absorb themselves in the subject matter, perhaps even experiencing a state of 'flow' or focused absorption (Csikszentmihalyi, 1990). There are countless examples where a typical structure of retrieval practice, direct instruction, student silent learning and then plenary might *not* be the best course of action or the most appropriate methodology for a single lesson, no matter how effective each of these elements may be as pedagogical practices. When teaching to the top, the key is to critically consider, before teaching each lesson, whether the lesson structure and pedagogical methods planned are the most appropriate to deliver highly challenging content. Lessons must be built on a foundation of strong subject knowledge, but learning itself can be structured in an innumerable variety of ways.

Unexpected directions and the benefits of responsive teaching

A flexible approach to structuring lessons and achieving learning objectives is not only something that can be planned into schemes of learning, but is also something that can – and indeed *should* – take place based on what happens in any particular lesson. In other words, a lesson can give us spontaneous learning opportunities to divert from our predetermined path, and to teach to the top by taking our lesson further than we had intended. As teachers, when we identify intellectual opportunities for integrating the highest-level knowledge, we should aim to grasp them rather than shy away from anything that takes us away from the lesson plan. Zazkis et al (2009:43) suggest a better alternative to prescriptive formats of lesson planning is 'interpretive' planning that allows for the 'different possibilities occasioned by a question or task, the different responses a student might offer, or conceptions a student might build'. There is a balance to be struck between covering the curriculum and knowing when, instead, to embrace unexpected opportunities to broaden knowledge or deepen a lesson's focus. The best way to achieve this is to plan for the long term rather than lesson by lesson.

Teachers in the classroom must work with 'fundamental uncertainty' from moment to moment (Heritage and Heritage, 2013:187) and effective teachers will respond to their students' learning needs by adjusting to help them reach learning aims. Effective teachers will construct their responses to students' answers to questioning with a kind of 'nimble understanding and constructive response that moves learning forward' (Heritage and Heritage, *ibid),* and teacher discretion and adaptability in adjusting the curriculum to their learners may make for more effective teaching (Allington et al, 2002). When it comes to differentiation by support for those struggling to access elements of a lesson, this is something that most experienced teachers do fluidly and efficiently. We know that we need to achieve the learning objectives for the lesson or the unit, and thus any good teacher will respond supportively and adaptably to students struggling with key elements. Yet this isn't always the case when it comes to expanding learning *beyond* the lesson aims or responding to unexpected avenues that present themselves during the lesson. Unexpected intellectual opportunities might be elicited either by students' responses to questions or by their questions to the teacher – these will often be moments where something you haven't anticipated comes to light and an opportunity for challenge presents itself. If you are determinedly following a lesson plan, it can be tempting to respond as briefly as possible in order to cram in the elements that you had pre-planned for your lesson and reach your final objective. While understandable, this can mean that key chances to embed higher-level subject knowledge beyond the curriculum are missed. Sometimes this can also be due to the anxieties elicited by teaching a subject with which one is less familiar, as teachers may be tempted to avoid discussion of areas in which they are lacking in confidence.

It is a mistake to shy away from changing our lesson plan if there is an opportunity to develop students' knowledge and push learning to a higher level. Responding extensively to a student's spontaneous question can provide unexpected opportunities to use the full extent of your subject knowledge, which in turn can help us to emphasise the value of knowledge in our classrooms. It can give pupils an idea of the breadth of exciting and interesting knowledge that exists in a discipline, even beyond the classroom or the curriculum. Sometimes, questions or unexpected directions can illuminate areas that you perhaps should have planned into the curriculum, but hadn't thought to. You can respond spontaneously during the lesson, and then reflect on how to adapt plans in future to encompass this element of knowledge in future learning.

Spontaneous discussions or responses can also lay the groundwork for further learning in the future.

So, if a discussion takes an unexpected turn, we should embrace that opportunity. The teacher who approaches every lesson with rigid timings and inflexibility is often less successful than the one who uses their subject knowledge and pedagogical skills to respond reflectively to the progress of a lesson. One of the unique challenges of teaching lies in the translation of high-level knowledge or expertise to the classroom. Teaching to the top means not shying away from sharing a concept or an idea because it is at the top of your knowledge base or is one of the more challenging aspects of the subject, and instead embracing this as an invaluable learning opportunity. Noticing unexpected opportunities by responding to questions and unexpected directions the lesson takes can take a kind of courage, as it means that teaching cannot always be reduced to a tick-list plan, but it is an approach for which the benefits pay off.

When we think about learning approaches as existing over time, we make space to deviate from the route we have set for ourselves and for students to conceptualise our subject as broader than any single test, assessment or learning objective. Whilst keeping the overall objective in mind, we need to take the time to recognise both *misconceptions* – and to take the time to work on these – and also learning *opportunities* to embed higher-level knowledge. Sometimes there can be surprising moments when students ask a question that takes you away from your lesson plan but is nevertheless important in a disciplinary sense. It may not be relevant to the specific lesson, but it is relevant to the subject – and it may be far better to spend time developing student knowledge in this area than to dismiss a pertinent question or learning opportunity simply for the purpose of rushing to the learning objective. While learning objectives are useful in terms of clarifying curriculum aims and directing students' attention to key content (Simon and Taylor, 2009; Wang et al, 2013), this does not mean that the learning objective or the specific lesson goal is the *only* thing that matters. Our subject itself and the panoply of unexpected learning opportunities it contains need to be valued as well, as they contribute to the fabric of understanding of the discipline as a whole. This is another reason why taking the opportunity to develop our subject knowledge prior to teaching topics is crucial if we are to be capable of responding reflectively to these unexpected learning opportunities.

While developing your subject knowledge will help you to adapt the lesson plan where needed and take intellectual autonomy in your own classroom, though, we need to accept that nobody can ever know everything. If a question throws us in terms of our existing subject knowledge, this is often a helpful indication that it is exactly the type of higher-level knowledge or conceptual understanding that is very much worth postponing part of our lesson for, or moving it to the next lesson. Some teachers feel judged or inadequate if they do not reach the planned end-point of their lesson, but reflective and responsive teaching *during* the lesson will mean that this inevitably sometimes occurs. If we are not too confident about the question asked or the subject matter, we can think *with* the students or even look up the concept or idea with them. In fact, it is a fantastic opportunity to show students that high-level knowledge does not necessarily mean 'Grade 9' or 'A' and that there are opportunities for learning existing at ever-deeper levels all around us. We can give them time to think about their question and also think about it ourselves. We can confess to the fact that it is a challenging question that we need some time to contemplate, and think together with the class about it, or research it with them on the computer. Such responses model the fact that challenge is intellectually exciting and not something to be avoided or feared. The teacher is the expert in the room, but any professional has their limits of expertise. Seeking out further information is a sign of perspicacity and reflectiveness rather than ignorance. Also, a readiness to explain areas you are less familiar with and share the discovery of new knowledge models an approach to learning that all students can benefit from.

You may ask, 'But what if we don't quite meet our objective during a lesson because I have spent so long responding to an unexpected question or idea? What if we spend so long talking about a concept largely unrelated to the lesson aims that we miss out a chunk of the intended learning?' It's a logical question because, as teachers, we have been trained to set an objective linked to the curriculum and reach it. My response would be, 'So what?' Curricula are not all-encompassing oracles that mandate *everything* students can or should ever learn. They are crucial, as they contain fundamental elements that children will learn and which will be built on, revisited and developed as students progress through their schooling. They must, therefore, be deeply considered, challenging and coherent (Myatt, 2018). Yet our expectations should also reach beyond the curriculum, no matter how challenging a scheme of work or medium-term plan may be. They cannot contain every possible word, concept or unexpected avenue for discussion or learning that may arise. We must remember that curricula are, at their core, subjective and ineluctably informed by ideology and opinions. As a policy document, the curriculum, with no visible author, attempts to speak with a single voice and to appear as a 'rigid and prescriptive' (Maisuria, 2005:147) or immovable framework. In fact, curricula are produced after inevitable collaboration and discussion between different contributors with differing opinions. The curriculum is a starting point but can never envision every possible learning opportunity presented by a particular topic. If it could, any subject in the world could be distilled to a six-week scheme of learning.

We must remember, then, that just because we haven't anticipated a certain question or lesson direction in a plan or scheme of learning, this doesn't mean it is unimportant. If your assessment is in the next couple of lessons, then understandably you may be less willing to veer away from the plan, which is fine – unexpected questions and learning opportunities can be returned to. Generally, though, it should be viewed as a mark of sound professional judgement to adapt your lesson plan because you want more time and space to focus on an unforeseen area of need, or to adapt the way you teach a key concept. In my own research (2016) I have used the philosopher Henri Lefebvre's 1991 theory of social space to analyse the enactment of the curriculum in the classroom, exploring the way that the curriculum is often taught and experienced quite differently in the 'lived space' of the classroom to how it is planned by policymakers. This is inevitable, as learning takes place in real spaces with real students, and we must be able to adapt the imaginary directions of our curriculum to the myriad contexts of learning.

For instance, in my lessons that have taken unexpected directions, I have given classes a brief introduction to key philosophical ideas; discussed reader-response theory with Year 8; and introduced Year 10 to feminist literary criticism, to name but a few. Each of these lessons held value for the students' long-term learning and expansion of powerful knowledge, even if it did not directly relate to the scheme of learning. After reflecting on the lesson and realising the value of the unplanned element of the lesson, you can ensure that you return to the concept or theory to make sure that it is embedded and supports long-term learning, as well. It's not the case that you need to throw in unexpected or unrelated knowledge all the time, but we mustn't be afraid of these opportunities where they do arise. Of course, this is an approach that requires nuance and I am not suggesting that if a student asks, 'What are you having for your dinner, Miss?' that I would segue into an unrelated discussion. (Well, unless I was incredibly hungry perhaps...) The point I am making, though, is that we must be unafraid to grasp these unexpected opportunities where they arise. We must be prepared to deal with moments of uncertainty if we want to enable our classes to reach for the top. Otherwise, we might miss out on some of the most exciting and awe-inspiring learning opportunities of all.

Reflecting on unexpected learning opportunities

After lessons veer in an unexpected direction, no matter how important or necessary the diversion, it is important to take the time to reflect critically on how and why we developed the learning in a spontaneous or improvisational way. David Tripp (1993) coined the concept of 'critical incidents' which can be used by teachers as a springboard for development. Critical incidents are usually pedagogical events or experiences in the classroom, which can then act as a starting point for teacher development as we reflect on these key moments. He emphasises that after critical incidents, teachers should engage in 'critical incident reflection' whereby they consider the relevance of the incident for them as teachers and its implications for their future practice. This 'incident' will not necessarily be an unusual or dramatic one but instead an important moment which is relevant and for which reflection can be beneficial for improving practice. The concept of critical incidents is usually applied generally to a range of pedagogical situations, but it is highly useful when thinking specifically about unexpected opportunities for subject knowledge development. Critical incidents for subject knowledge development (either your own, or pupils') might be unexpected moments where you can challenge students by going beyond the curriculum or moments when you realise that there is a gap in your knowledge that only comes to light during the process of teaching something.

After a lesson, we can explore what our critical subject knowledge moments were, and why. We might reflect on whether there were any moments where we could have pushed students further, and on which element of higher-level knowledge we might teach differently next time. We may ask whether we needed to give an unplanned response to students' questions which pushed our knowledge to its limits, or whether there is a gap in the curriculum or our knowledge base that we only identified during the process of teaching. We might ask questions such as the following:

- Was there an opportunity to use subject knowledge that we hadn't expected, and would we apply the same knowledge again?
- Was a question asked that we didn't know the answer to? Is this an important area for us to develop depth of knowledge in order to teach to the top to a greater extent, next time we teach this topic?
- Has an element of knowledge arisen that you should embed into upcoming lessons in order to reinforce or clarify it?
- Do future lessons need to be adapted due to the time you took 'off-plan' today?

In other words, it's great to go off course in order to enrich the learning journey for your students and give them a richer educational experience. But to maximise the efficacy of this process, do ensure that you take the time after a lesson like this to reflect on the benefits of the learning, the ways that it can be embedded and developed going forwards, and on how you will ensure that you cover the curriculum too.

QUESTIONS FOR REFLECTION

- Think about a lesson or scheme of learning you have taught recently. Did any critical incidents for subject knowledge development arise during the process of teaching?
- When have spontaneous learning opportunities presented themselves in your lessons? Which of these has been the richest and most productive?
- Do you feel comfortable going beyond the curriculum in your discussions and explanations, where the opportunity arises? If not, what could make you feel more comfortable with this?
- When has it been helpful to adjust your plan 'ad hoc' during the lesson?
- Is your mindset fixed on student progress during a single lesson, or do you think about progress and learning over time?
- If you are a leader, are you tempted to jump to negative conclusions if you go into a classroom and observe a lesson in which the teacher hasn't reached the plenary, or in which the starter is still on a board? Or do you take the time to explore whether unexpected learning or productive discussion may have slowed the outward progress or 'pace' of a lesson?
- What are your own areas of expertise you can utilise to help you veer 'off-plan' if necessary?

Chapter 7

Creative approaches in the high challenge classroom

'Wisdom is not a product of schooling but of the lifelong attempt to acquire it.' – Albert Einstein

---

Resisting dichotomies, seeking balance

I want to preface this chapter by confessing that – as many of my friends would attest – I talk a lot. Both in life and in the classroom. I try to be a good listener too but I am sure any of the colleagues who have had the dubious pleasure of teaching in classrooms next door to me over the years could tell you that I do like to talk. I like explaining things, communicating clearly, telling stories that relate to our learning, and even occasionally making my students laugh. When I was once told in a meeting that we were to try to have less 'teacher talk' in our lessons, I admit that I declared: 'You can pry my teacher talk from my cold, dead hands.' (Yes, I can be a little too direct.) It's important to tell you this personal detail because I want my readers to know that I recognise the value of sometimes simply *telling* students things. Clear explanations, given with examples and opportunities for students to apply their learning, can – in my view – often be one of the most effective ways of teaching.

My own support for explicit explanations and 'teacher talk' does need to be stated because in this chapter I outline how we can both teach to the top and also make space for students' voices and ideas in the classroom. Some readers might assume that writing a chapter about students' voices and creative approaches to teaching means positioning myself in ideological opposition to teacher-led instruction. This is principally because, in recent years, a distinction has been drawn by some commentators between progressive and traditionalist pedagogical methods. In a 2014 blog post on his website 'Teacher Head', Tom Sherrington suggests that the divisions drawn in some quarters between methods seen as traditionalist (such as guided instruction and probing questioning) and progressive methods (such as enquiry learning or group work) have perhaps become entrenched due to both groups feeling they have to defend themselves against the other. Elements of teaching viewed as more traditional such as 'teacher talk' have arguably been unfairly denigrated over the years, with the expertise of teachers dismissed by senior leaders or Ofsted who previously insisted on entirely 'student-led' lessons. In contrast, those advocating for methods seen as more 'progressive' have been pushed to be defensive of their teaching in recent years due to their methods being seen as lacking rigour.

It is unhelpful and inaccurate to draw a binary distinction between progressivist and traditional methods, or direct instruction and other forms of learning as knowledge-rich and knowledge-poor. We should be careful not to entirely align one aspect of pedagogy with teaching to the top because the translation of high-level concepts and knowledge to the classroom can take place in a wide range of ways. Head of Policy at the EEF Robbie Coleman (2017) suggests, for example, that a class who receives a large amount of direct instruction at the beginning of a unit may, for instance, develop more independence as a unit progresses while instruction might be more teacher-led towards the beginning of a scheme of learning. Whole class explanations are a key feature of my own teaching and teacher-led instruction and its associations with a challenging curriculum are well-established (Stockard et al, 2018). I do not cover explicit teaching and explanations in this book in detail because a wealth of books already exist by practitioners covering these very topics in relation to challenging students to succeed (see, for example, Sherrington and Caviglioli's 2020 *Teaching WalkThrus: Five-step guide to instructional coaching* for excellent explanations of live modelling, worked examples, and metacognitive talk, to name but a few.)

The Department for Education seems to see direct instruction as inherently more 'knowledge-rich', for example with their grants to curriculum pilot programme being specifically intended to develop curricula that are 'knowledge-rich, and have teacher-led instruction and whole-class teaching at their core' (2018:6). Only certain forms of pedagogical methods are aligned with knowledge in the DfE's vision of the curriculum, which sees knowledge-rich classrooms are full of direct instruction, regular testing and spaced retrieval. Again, I want to stress here that I absolutely do not dispute that such methods can be a valid and worthy aspect of high-challenge teaching. But many of the best teachers use a plethora of pedagogical techniques, and I would argue that the division or categorisation of teaching in a binary way is reductive and detracts from our capacity to make nuanced decisions for each lesson depending on the content we are teaching. Pedagogical methods that might allow students to be creative, to be independent, to question, and to use their voices are highly valuable. A wonderfully challenging lesson can contain both traditional and progressive methods, and a scheme of learning over time might contain a myriad of different types of teaching, all of which can be pitched at the top level. A classroom where you are teaching to the top may certainly include such techniques viewed by some as 'traditionalist', such as:

- Clear, explicit and direct instruction or mini-lectures from the teacher
- Teacher-led questioning
- Independent silent working
- Quizzes
- Retention-based activities such as call and response
- Teacher-led analysis of pre-prepared model answers

But it could also contain, as I explore in this chapter:

- Student-centred discussion
- Whole class discussion that aims to be more 'dialogic' and to incorporate students' voices as much as – or even more than – the teacher's
- Giving time for student research with presentations on learning
- Encouraging creative representations of the subject matter, or embodied learning or dramatic activities

All the strategies outlined above can be effective in different circumstances and, in fact, the latter methods can be more 'knowledge-rich' than the former, depending on how learning is framed. For example, direct instruction can be less effective in some circumstances if it is based on inadequate subject knowledge, pitched too low, poorly planned, or inappropriate to the topic area (Eppley and Dudley-Marling, 2019) – even, perhaps, if it is taught by someone who is so unengaging in their style of delivery that students drift off! Similarly, retrieval practice – or any other pedagogical method currently seen as research-informed and *de rigeur* – can be ineffective if not implemented at a challenging level. The danger with a polarised discourse around pedagogy is that more creative and discourse-led approaches have been characterised as less aspirational when, in fact, any type of teaching can fall into the trap of teaching to the bottom or the middle, and failing to challenge students. There is no need to state that we are committed *either* to direct instruction or a child-centred approach and the two do not need to be viewed as diametrically opposed philosophies.

Challenging students through dialogic learning

In the classroom, we often do not place enough importance on talk. Barbara Bleiman argues that dialogue is 'as complicated as writing' (2021) but whilst we frequently recognise the importance of writing in different contexts in school, we often neglect consideration of the different contexts of talk and the value of talk for learning. Sinclair and Coulthard's seminal work in classroom discourse analysis (1975) indicated that much classroom dialogue revolved around an initiation-response-feedback pattern where the teacher asks a question (initiating an exchange), the student responds, and then the teacher provides feedback, as in 'yes' or 'not quite'. There are instances when the use of this pattern makes sense, such as when recapping information or in retrieval practice, but at other times it can mean that we do not enable students to fully develop their ideas.

The extensive research of Robin Alexander has indicated that this questioning pattern can lead to closed, one-word answers, acting as a 'cognitively-restricting ritual' (Alexander, 2006:14) if it is embedded in classroom practice. Language, as well as representing our thoughts, helps us to construct ideas (Alexander, 2008:92) and 'talk mediates the cognitive and cultural spaces between adult and child, among children themselves, between teacher and learner, between society and the individual' (Alexander, 2008:9). Alexander's research is supported by that of Neil Mercer who argues that talk can provide a means of collective reasoning (2019). In other words, through making room for extended and structured dialogue in the classroom, we can more easily bridge the gap between the learner and what is to be learned, as well as giving students opportunities to think deeply and in extended ways around a topic. According to the Education Endowment Foundation, dialogic methods seek to enable students to 'reason, discuss, argue and explain rather than merely respond' and to develop 'higher order thinking and articulacy' (EEF, 2020). Their recent review of dialogic teaching found that primary school pupils taught using dialogic methods made on average two months additional progress in English, maths and science, compared to control groups.

With dialogic learning, we can seek to have more extended, developed discussions around a particular topic, perhaps by asking a more challenging, conceptually difficult question and then providing students with support to develop detailed verbal responses. Such structured dialogue can take place on a whole class basis, in pairs, or in small groups. 'Group work' is sometimes denigrated as a tool of pedagogy in the 'knowledge-rich' classroom. At the time of writing, I have just read the knowledge-rich curriculum statement of an academy trust (to remain anonymous here) which discourages group work in favour of a narrow range of other methods that it now states are more 'research-based'. Group work *can* be done badly – like any pedagogical method. Often, 'group work gone wrong' might involve minimal framing from the teacher, leading to students' conversations veering off-topic. But any pedagogical method can be implemented badly and if we resist all forms of group work simply because this *can* be practised poorly, we risk abandoning a highly useful opportunity for developing critical thought. To counter the potential for group discussion to be ineffective, we can provide students with rules or a clear structure for classroom talk. Critical, exploratory discussion can be difficult so providing a framework for students can 'represent a kind of freedom' (Mercer et al, 2004:375) rather than a constraint, providing them with the tools to converse deeply around a topic.

When facilitating effective peer or classroom discussion, we might provide phrases such as:

- *One criticism of your viewpoint could be...*
- *I agree that... however...*
- *I would develop this point further by...*
- *The aspect of your argument I most agree with is...*
- *The point I agreed with the least was...*
- *Some people might agree that... but ....*

It can also be useful to provide students with opportunities to develop their ideas or arguments individually before sharing their ideas with the group, or to reflect on a resource before the discussion, in order to ensure confidence in participation. Well-planned talk can be eminently knowledge-rich, and helps us move away from an IRF pattern and towards a richer level of discourse. Most universities employ a mixture of expert-led lectures and deeper student engagement with subject matter in the form of seminars; a balance of expertise and the opportunity to discuss, reflect and debate can, likewise, be eminently beneficial for learners in schools.

Challenging questioning

Alongside championing dialogic learning and more extended, reflective discourse in the classroom, we can use the technique known as Socratic questioning to help talk go further, a practice inspired by Plato's account of the way Socrates used focused yet open questions to help his interlocutor construct knowledge. The Socratic method of questioning refers to asking leading questions to help students construct an understanding of the subject matter; it involves the teacher modelling a process of wondering aloud, expressing areas of ignorance and intellectual curiosity. It also may involve asking questions without necessarily always having a clear idea of one right answer (Hunkins, 1989); questions that might be spontaneous, based on students' responses, but can also be planned (Paul and Elder, 2008). The use of Socratic questioning can allow students to apply the concepts of critical, exploratory questioning to their own thinking, and the spontaneous discussions that arise can also 'provide models of listening critically as well as exploring the beliefs expressed' (Paul and Elder, 2008:34).

In the strictest sense, the Socratic dialectic would involve a discussion entirely constructed around the questioner asking a long series of questions to reach an eventual end-point (Paul and Elder, 2008) and might also involve providing the class with minimal information or input before questioning. While this can occasionally be appropriate, I tend to prefer Socratic-*inspired* questioning, integrating questions that challenge students' preconceptions or ask them to justify their thinking at key points in the lesson, using them at points where it is important to develop an understanding of key concepts or to reflect on presuppositions. For example, Socratic-inspired questions might involve teachers asking students to clarify their reasoning by giving evidence or explanations, such as by asking:

- 'Why do you think that?'
- 'What has led you to that conclusion?'
- 'Why might someone else disagree with you?'
- 'Who might feel differently about this?'

A caveat here is that a Socratic questioning style must be positively framed and employed with a sense of respect for the self-esteem of the student, as an insistence on deconstructing the origins of their beliefs could potentially feel quite alarming or even humiliating for students not accustomed to this style of questioning. Proceed with caution, then, but do proceed because, if enacted in a positively framed way, Socratic questioning can help us to illuminate the root of misconceptions or misapprehensions, alongside guiding students to clarify their own thinking. The psychological notion of belief perseverance suggests that existing beliefs resist changing and take time to challenge. Individuals tend to hold on to what they already believe, even when given new information that does not support this view (Burbules and Linn,

1992). Socratic questioning can help students to develop their ability to interrogate their own beliefs and understanding, as well as to develop their ability to think deeply.

Through questioning more broadly, we can build interactions that help us co-construct concepts and build cognition. Even in Early Years settings, learning takes place through a process of shared concept-building, or 'sustained shared thinking' (Siraj-Blatchford et al, 2002). We can use the same concept in the high challenge classroom, using questioning to work *with* our students to develop their understanding. This can sometimes be achieved through rapid question and answer sessions but, to achieve depth of thought and to allow students to grapple with more challenging concepts, it can be preferable to ask more difficult questions with longer wait times (Cohen et al, 2004). According to Martin Robinson (2013), a challenging curriculum – and thus, by extension, a lesson – should allow space for students to be able to think, criticise and be sceptical. Questioning is a vital tool for achieving that.

Counterfactual thinking

Counterfactual questioning, or 'what if' questions, can also be a valuable way of stimulating deep thought. For instance, in history, we might ask 'what if' a particular incident hadn't occurred, which then helps students to interrogate the consequences and impact of historical events. Or what if we didn't have access to a particular primary source? How would that change our perspective? In geography, we might ask what if a certain natural disaster hadn't occurred, or what if the population of a particular country had remained static? In maths, what if we had used a different process to work out the answer, or we alter one element of the formula? In English, what if the poet had used a different type of structure? How would this alter the meaning? Or what if the story had a different narrator, or the writer had used a different word here, or there?

Such contemplation of alternatives, possibilities and even impossibilities is not likely to be tested explicitly on an exam. However, exploration of what has *not* happened by imagining counterfactual possibilities is a simple way of illuminating the consequences of choices. If we are to truly teach to the top, we must allow room for wondering, contemplation and musing, which facilitates breadth as well as depth of thought. Similarly, we can encourage criticality by presenting students with contestable or questionable opinions and providing them with opportunities to debate the opposite viewpoint, or asking them to argue the reverse of their own viewpoint. It stands to reason that the more we argue about difficult concepts, the less intimidating or challenging this is to do in the future; it is important to give students opportunities to 'work the muscle' of academic argument to make it stronger. Arguing allows us to look at situations and concepts from multiple angles, which is the essence of critical thinking.

Students as questioners, researchers and presenters

Accordingly, alongside working on the challenging questions we devise for our classes – both planned and spontaneous – we can also give students the opportunities to be the questioners. Students are, of course, usually the 'answerers' in a classroom, but the opportunity to devise their own questions (questions which go beyond clarification of the teachers' meaning) can be beneficial for learning (King, 1989; Gunn, 2008). Questioning is a thinking processing skill which is 'structurally embedded in […] critical thinking, creative thinking, and problem solving' (Cuccio-Schirripa and Steiner, 2000). Therefore, by giving students challenging material or resources and then giving them the time and space to ask questions, we enable them to both encounter high-challenge content but, at the same time, develop their ability to think critically.

To make this process easier, teachers can provide a model for questioning by talking through their own thought process and how they came to ask a particular question (Fordham, 2006) and exemplify how to extend and develop one's own thinking through questioning. When we demonstrate questioning techniques, we help students to develop their own ability to ask complex questions and can help them acquire metacognitive strategies to enable them to reflect on their own existing understanding of a topic (Lewin, 2010).

In practice, assigning 'students as questioners' might work in the classroom by providing them with a challenging resource, such as a historical source, explanation of a scientific process, or a poem, and simply asking them: What questions do you have? The richness and range of students' questions can be surprising and can often illuminate exactly what you would wish to teach them anyway. They have, in the process of asking questions, drawn out important details themselves and developed their ability to think critically. If needed, we could also provide students with question stems or give models of different types of questions. Giving students challenging material and then affording them the opportunity to formulate questions about it has also been shown to improve their ability to respond themselves to higher order questions (Aflalo, 2021). Many of us in the world of classroom teaching have experienced situations where certain more confident or highly attaining students ask perspicacious and insightful questions. So, facilitating opportunities for *all* students, even if initially reluctant, to ask thoughtful questions is a fantastic way to increase challenge for everyone in the classroom. Even more importantly, by making questioning an integral part of the learning experience, it may help to ensure that students are inspired through their experience of learning to never stop seeking out knowledge and understanding.

Similarly, we can give opportunities for students to develop their independence by allowing – often after some initial input – time for independent research and working towards presenting on topics, in much the same way as learning might take place at university level. Depending on the subject you teach, you could assign high-level concepts, ideas or elements of the curriculum plan to small groups or individual students, with learning kept focused by giving students the end-point or objective of presenting their findings to the class in a subsequent lesson. If we truly want to teach to the top, we should think about how learning will take place beyond the school gates. While teaching only using direct instruction can enable good exam results, this should be balanced with other approaches if we are going to provide our students with the best preparation for A Level and university study, as well as the world of work.

Creativity and teaching to the top

As students move through their schooling and towards their final examinations, they will usually have fewer and fewer opportunities to engage in activities we might categorise as 'creative' in any meaningful sense. Creativity is difficult to measure, and there is no one agreed definition of what 'counts' as creativity in the classroom (Karwowski et al, 2020). However, students' ability to be creative and academic success are correlated (Gajda et al, 2017), and, therefore, we might wish to harness opportunities for creativity that will also enable us to challenge our students. In psychology, creativity has been found to co-exist with greater tolerance of ambiguity or uncertainty (Zenasni et al, 2008), and being capable of exploring different perspectives, situations or topics from multiple angles is a key element of thinking critically and deeply. Thus, employing an element of creativity in our teaching and giving students opportunities to be creative may help them to develop an increased capacity to analyse and deconstruct information by viewing situations from different perspectives.

Spaces for creativity lie in our curriculum content, even if these are not referred to explicitly. In my research, I have explored the creative potential within policy (Mansworth, 2016) which, as teachers, we can unveil, manipulate and expose in the classroom. Creative approaches should not be seen as woolly, indefinable elements that only aim to 'increase creativity' or which have unclear objectives. In fact, students seem to find it easier to be most creative when clear constraints and guidelines are given, such as time limits, word limits, and provision of clear objectives and parameters (Rawling and Westaway, 2003). For example, in history, students might devise their own propaganda posters in order to apply the elements of propaganda and thus more effectively remember them, or write creative newspaper articles from the perspective of a person experiencing a historical event. In English, students might apply their understanding of the features of poetry by using them in their own poems or devise an additional scene for the Shakespeare play they are studying which aims to develop an important theme. The use of creative approaches can give students an opportunity to consolidate advanced knowledge and can also be useful in helping students to remember and understand concepts by applying them.

Depending on the subject matter, we can also creatively use the body as a resource for making meaning in lessons. In English, when learning new grammatical concepts, gesture can help to support understanding by making the implicit more explicit (Giovanelli, 2015b) or we ask students to freeze frame or physically represent concepts, ideas or texts to draw out different potential meanings of texts (Mansworth, 2016). Creative approaches do not need to be lengthy processes that take up the majority of the lesson but rather, a single challenging lesson might involve a mixture of creative and traditional approaches, with the creative elements used to support the teaching of conceptually challenging content. Creativity also does not need to involve the construction of something tangible but can mean the construction of new meanings and interpretations as the teacher provides questions with more than one possible answer. It can be found even in the encouragement of exploratory responses or in a teacher sometimes allowing discussions to deviate from a set path and to veer in unexpected, yet productive, directions. As an additional benefit, using creative approaches can mean that the student in the class who is not necessarily the highest achiever academically can have a rare chance, through engaging in alternative modes of expression, to be the most successful student in the room, thus helping to facilitate the development of students' self-esteem levels and enthusiasm for learning.

Creative activities can also afford us the opportunity to exploit the power of the emotions. Psychological research has indicated that emotional events are remembered more clearly than non-emotional events; emotion facilitates encoding and retrieval (Tyng et al, 2017) and words associated with emotion are recalled better than neutral words (Khairudin et al, 2012). Whilst in the past, emotions were viewed as somehow *interfering* with cognition, more recent research shows that emotions are actually integral to cognition and therefore to learning (Zull, 2006). The experience of emotion and cognition is supported by interdependent neural processes (Immordino-Yang and Damasio, 2007) and emotions are so integral to learning that it is 'neurobiologically impossible to build memories, engage complex thoughts, or make meaningful decisions without emotions' (Immordino-Yang, 2016:18). The emotional aspects of pedagogy in the classroom are rarely discussed, but a wealth of psychological research on the emotions and cognition would suggest that activities that engage students emotionally may help ensure the retention of information, alongside facilitating students' ability to think deeply and to apply learning to different contexts. It is common for English teachers to include activities that involve writing or speaking in role from the perspective of different characters or from alternative viewpoints in their lessons, but this is an empathy-developing technique that can also feasibly be adapted to other subjects. For example, an activity such as writing a tabloid article about a historical event or writing from the point of view of someone affected by a particular geographical case study could be useful in helping students to develop emotional connection with a topic and remember it better in the future, as long as they are directed to include key elements which are appropriate to their learning. As an additional bonus, empathy is positively correlated with academic success (Feshbach and Feshbach, 2009). So, any activity that helps build empathy is worth doing on an academic level, as well as – of course – being quite likely to help contribute to our students' development as caring, compassionate individuals, which – while not the focus of this book – is surely inextricable from our role as teachers.

QUESTIONS FOR REFLECTION

- Think about a lesson you have taught recently. Could it be possible for the whole class discussion element to be more dialogic? How? How could elements be adapted to extend students' contributions?
- Where do you use an initiation-response-feedback method in your own teaching? Where does this work well? At which points would a different structure be preferable?
- When looking at your schemes of work, which are the elements of your lesson that might benefit most from a direct instruction (or 'traditionalist') approach, and which might benefit from the incorporation of other methods?
- Where and how could aspects of Socratic questioning work in your teaching? Are there any topics or areas of the curriculum it could lend itself well to?
- Look at one of your curriculum or lesson plans. Are there any points at which counterfactual thinking (or 'what if?') questions could be included? What could be the benefits of this for your subject?
- In *your* subject, which elements or creative approaches could be applicable?
- Are there any curriculum elements that could be adapted to engage students emotionally or provide opportunities for empathetic engagement?
- Where could you build in opportunities for students to act as questioners in your classroom?

Chapter 8

Giving students the confidence to reach for the top

'How powerful would our world be if we had kids who were not afraid to take risks, who were not afraid to think, and who had a champion?' – Rita Pierson

---

Self-esteem and self-perception

'Miss', frowned one of my Year 11s last year, in response to an explanation I had just given about awe, wonder and the sublime in relation to Wordsworth's *The Prelude*, 'Is there any point in me listening to this if my target is a Grade 4?' I explained to the student in this case that, actually, learning about the concept could be really interesting and useful beyond their exam – alongside possibly helping them to achieve a higher grade. Yet my response was essentially ineffective as I was really just dealing with the surface question, as we all often have to do in a busy classroom. I wasn't responding to the root question at all; this student was asking something far deeper and more entrenched. When students ask, 'Is there any point in this?' often they are actually saying something else. They are asking: Do I deserve and need this type of knowledge? Am I the type of person who should have access to these ideas? Is this knowledge or level of learning something I can cope with? I call these 'challenge-resistant responses' and teachers encounter them particularly when introducing new or challenging topics. The expressing of such attitudes and such resistance by our students usually does not indicate that students are inherently afraid of hard work, or even that unfamiliar concepts bore, perturb or confuse them. Instead, when students react with dislike or annoyance towards a new topic, idea or challenging concept, it may indicate that they have developed an internalised negative self-image limiting their own perception of what they can know and understand.

This self-perception of one's own abilities and intellectual capacity is sometimes called academic self-concept by psychologists and researchers. Academic self-concept originates in the work of the renowned psychotherapist Carl Rogers on self-concept more generally (1959) which refers to the collection of beliefs one has about oneself and is constituted of three elements: self-image, or the opinion one has of oneself; self-esteem, or how much value one places on oneself; and, the ideal self, or what one wishes one were like. When students are still in primary school, and in some cases as early as between ages 3 to 5 (Tiedemann, 2000), they develop an academic self-concept relating to how competent or clever they think they are in comparison to their peers (Rubie-Davies, 2006). A study by Chevalier et al (2009) found that high school pupils with a more positive perception of their own academic abilities were more likely to expect to go to university even after controlling for attainment and students' characteristics, whereas multiple research studies have indicated a correlation between academic self-concept and performance (Chen et al, 2013; Marsh and Craven, 2006). However, our academic self-concept is not necessarily based on fact and self-estimates of ability are often likely to be inaccurate (Freund and Kasten, 2012). Sometimes, the way we see ourselves may actually have a more significant effect on our capacity to succeed than our actual ability. So, we end up with a situation whereby students judge their own ability in relation to their peers as early as pre-school and these beliefs may then be continually reinforced as they progress through primary and secondary school.

If we think about the student asking me 'Is there any point in me listening to this?' when I introduced a more challenging interpretation of Wordsworth's poem than they had been introduced to previously, we can infer that – in all likelihood – their academic self-concept is unlikely to be high, and they are thus more reluctant to tackle tasks or even consider ideas or concepts they consider to be academically challenging. The result? Lower achievement, reinforcing lower academic self-concept, which in turn leads to lower achievement. Research by Guay et al (2003) found that academic self-concept has an effect on academic achievement and academic achievement then has an effect on self-concept. We can easily end up with a vicious circle whereby negative academic self-concept leads to lower levels of achievement, which then obviously reinforce students' pre-existing beliefs, thus leading to worse achievement in the future. The consequences of low academic self-concept for pupils such as the Year 11 mentioned above are enormous. For learners with low academic self-concept, approaching new information and difficult topics is inherently more difficult than it is for others, even if the problem is largely in their heads rather than existing in reality. For teachers, the attitudes and ingrained beliefs of pupils like this can, unsurprisingly, makes teaching to the top even more challenging, as alongside the practical task of making high-level knowledge or concepts come alive in our classroom, we also need to attempt to redress some of the harms caused by these students' pre-existing beliefs.

As I discussed in Chapter 5, the problematic practices of differentiation by setting and by task can contribute to this internalised belief, but lack of confidence in tackling challenging content – or, as in the case of the student above, even listening to my explanation – may also have a plethora of other contributing factors. Self-esteem is a predictor of academic achievement (Aryana, 2010; Roman et al, 2008), and it is a sad but true fact that some of our children have been taught or have learned in some way to see themselves as 'less than' and have developed low self-esteem before they even set foot in our classroom. Sometimes this might be caused by previous self-perceived failures and sometimes their internalised self-perception might pervade all their subjects. Whatever the cause, children with either low self-esteem more generally or low academic self-concept will be far less likely to reach for the top in *any* form – and may potentially even engage in harmful or learning-resistant behaviours. For instance, an ethnographic study of black students in an American high school found that subcultures of resistance developed as a reaction to feeling alienated by learning (Mac an Ghaill, 1988). The answer isn't to avoid teaching children high-level knowledge but to increase their self-confidence in order to help harness the belief that this is knowledge *for them* and that they have the capability to reach for the top in their learning.

Breaking the academic self-concept vicious circle: high challenge, high encouragement

Research has indicated that self-concept – more generally – is malleable, with our self-concept changing and adjusting depending on the social situation and our experiences (Markus and Kunda, 1986). It is not a huge leap to hypothesise that academic self-concept may also be malleable. Any teacher who has watched a child grow in confidence or develop a more positive attitude when approaching a task or an idea can testify to this. Byrne (1990) distinguished between academic self-concept and general self-concept, with her research suggesting that academic self-concept had a greater impact on students' achievement than general self-concept. When students achieve, then their self-confidence and academic self-concept is likely to improve (Guay et al, 2003). While students' general self-concept and self-esteem is important, building their academic self-concept specifically may be key to improving their achievement.

So, how can we help students to develop their confidence to reach for the top in their learning and to believe that all knowledge should be accessible to them and that their grades, targets or previous achievement shouldn't determine the learning they deserve? For a pupil with low academic self-concept, our priority needs to be altering their self-image and self-perception of their abilities and capacity to tackle challenges in the long term, through the way we frame learning and boost their self-confidence in our subject on a day-to-day basis. It is unlikely to be possible to achieve this in one lesson or day; whatever I said to my Year 11 student, I probably would find it difficult to increase their academic self-concept instantly. What is needed is a long term, continual commitment on the part of the teacher to increasing students' academic self-concept, which will then have a knock-on effect on their achievement in the subject and may even feed into a more self-assured approach to other subjects too.

The best approach to building students' confidence levels is simply to believe in them. We need to strike a careful balance between high challenge and high encouragement in our lessons in order to increase their academic self-concept in our subject. Alongside setting high expectations for the children we teach, we need to champion their ability to take risks, even if these risks are just opening their minds to new or high-level ideas, or trying out a task that seems very challenging at first. The answer is not to reduce the challenge or the anticipated level of outcome, as students need to be given challenges in order to realise they can meet them. Even if they initially resist, we can continue to present them with challenges as long as this is balanced with an attitude of support, encouragement and believing they can do it. The combination of continual challenge *and* encouragement is crucial because praising children *without* a high level of challenge can be entirely counterproductive and feasibly harmful to their academic self-concept. Amemiya and Wang (2018) suggest that praising for effort can inadvertently backfire in adolescence, as lower attaining pupils can perceive the praise as patronising or can view it as implying that the student needs to work hard because of low innate ability.

This is where we need to tread carefully around Dweck's concept of growth mindset (2008) which has sometimes been misinterpreted as suggesting students should be praised *only* for effort, as in their teacher writing 'Good try' or 'Good effort' on their work. Haimovitz and Dweck (2017) caution that, in fact, the research does not suggest that children should be praised purely for effort, but instead that teachers should tie the process – as in their effort – to the outcome. By contrast to 'Good effort', an example of praise encompassing effort and outcome might be 'You have worked so hard to develop your understanding of catharsis and your essay shows such thoughtful integration of these ideas.' Dweck's highly influential concept of growth mindset can help us to remember to instil a belief in children that their effort is what makes a difference rather than any inherent ability, but teachers should be cautious about the *way* they praise. Haimovitz and Dweck (2017) also suggest that praising just for effort can inadvertently imply that the onus for improving learning is entirely on students' efforts alone; they suggest instead that a goal for educators could be to foster a sense of shared responsibility for learning in their classes to 'help students to appraise setbacks not as indicative of their own personal shortcomings' and to see difficulties and challenges as a key part of learning (2017:1855). For example, we can acknowledge the complexity of an idea, but share our excitement about ways it can be applied effectively or how we could use it in the future.

In earlier chapters, I have discussed support in the form of differentiation, but support can also come in the form of emotional support. Our students need to be challenged to think, but this is best achieved in a classroom with a teacher who cares about them. In other words, the warmer we are, the kinder we are, and the more positive we are, the more we can get children who have lower academic and general self-concept to feel capable of facing challenges, whether that's just listening to a new idea or applying new approaches. We need to make our children feel supported, we need to make them feel they can succeed, and then they will be able to achieve. The educator Rita Pierson, quoted at the start of this chapter, said in her now-famous 2013 Ted Talk that 'every child needs a champion'. In other words, all children need someone on their side, someone who believes in them and expects the best from them. Positive relationships between students and teachers have been found to have a positive impact on children's success in school as well as their engagement (Hamre and Pianta, 2006; Roorda et al, 2011). By balancing high levels of challenge with a high amount of encouragement, we can ensure that students feel that we believe they can achieve great things but that we will support them to get there. We can build encouragement and championing of our students into our interactions with them throughout their lessons.

Effective ways to do this are innumerable, but here are some examples of interactions or instances that might demonstrate a balance between high challenge and high encouragement:

- Show that you notice and remember what they do well. This can be especially effective when done publicly and almost off-hand – catching students off-guard and therefore avoiding some of the pitfalls associated with immediate praise. For example, a seemingly quick and casual comment such as: 'Oh yes – and Sam made an excellent point linking to that last lesson, didn't he?', or 'You could use an extended metaphor Jo, you did that really well in your creative piece.' Showing that you *remember and value* students' achievements and are pleased by them is invaluable for making students realise you believe in them and that they are important in your classroom. Psychological research has shown that unexpected positive feedback increases motivation (Deci, 1971).

- Try using 'we' pronouns rather than 'you'. This is highly beneficial as a way to frame learning because it helps foster the sense of a shared learning journey explored by Haimovitz and Dweck (2017). For example, 'We have made some amazing progress in our extended essay responses', or 'I was just blown away by the way some of us have managed to include so much of the sophisticated vocabulary in our responses.'
- Positively highlight where students have used high-level concepts or met challenges using your visualiser, displays or just verbally. Get excited about this and let students feel your excitement and enthusiasm.
- Foster a warm climate in your classroom. Teacher and psychologist Haim Ginott said: 'I have come to a frightening conclusion. I am the decisive element in the classroom. It is my personal approach that creates the climate.' (1972:15) If you create a sunny and positive climate of praise, happiness and warmth, students will feel they can take risks. They know they will never be ridiculed or humiliated, and they will feel able to risk falling because they know they will be able to get up again.
- Continually highlight students' strengths. While it's important to be able to give feedback and areas for improvement, ensure that these are counterbalanced with emphasis on the positive.
- Begin lessons with 'success starters'. Open with easily accessible questions or tasks to embed confidence and can-do attitude. These can be open enough to enable everyone to participate at the same time as allowing for higher-level responses.
- Use supportive differentiation to make it very hard to fail. Give thinking time, scaffold and support, in order to avoid students experiencing too much failure. While earlier in this book I discuss 'desirable difficulties' (Bjork and Bjork, 2011), these cannot be at the expense of students' self-esteem. Provide the challenging content but do not make it possible to 'get stuck' for long.
- Prioritise quality over quantity and depth over breadth. This means slowing down explanations and not overloading students' working memories. High challenge does not need to mean crammed with content.

- Paradoxically, ample scaffolding and support to access challenging resources breed autonomy as students feel empowered and confident to tackle them alone.
- Afford students the time and space to work independently in some lessons, but after ample preparation for this.
- Give students the opportunity to make a contribution in the classroom such as by preparing a presentation linked to the curriculum – again, provide support to ensure they are well-prepared with the tools for success and praise their achievement.

Increasing motivation alongside confidence

Alongside building students' confidence to increase their academic self-concept, it can also be helpful to consider academic research on motivation and to consider how we can better motivate students to aim for 'the top' and to not shy away from challenging tasks or concepts. According to Deci and Ryan's 'self-determination theory' (1985) three basic psychological needs contribute to motivation: autonomy, competence and relatedness. Competence refers to both people's genuine ability but also their belief in their own competence. Autonomy means feeling a level of control over our own goals and a sense of being able to act independently, whilst relatedness means our ability and opportunity to interact with and be connected to others.

In the classroom, this triad could feasibly help us to increase student self-determination and their motivation to tackle challenging content:

- To generate autonomy in the classroom, we can work to enable students to feel in control of their own achievement by giving them the resources and support to succeed.
- Competence goes hand in hand with the methods for increasing academic self-concept outlined above – making students feel successful will increase their sense of competence.
- Relatedness is encapsulated in the way we treat students and the atmosphere we cultivate in our classes.

These strategies for increasing motivation are in many ways very similar to and interact with strategies used for increasing confidence, self-esteem and academic self-concept. Following the strategies outlined in the previous section is likely to increase both confidence *and* motivation. In many ways, these go hand in hand, but it is important to remember that increasing student motivation is important *in conjunction* with carefully considering the content of the learning: 'Learning requires motivation, but motivation does not necessarily lead to learning.' (Nuthall, 2007:35) So, as emphasised throughout this book, teaching to the top remains crucial. We must balance our lesson content with consideration of the individuals in our classes and reflection on how we can best enable them to engage positively with the learning and reach for the top both with confidence and motivation.

Students are happier within their comfort zone than when they are faced with new ideas (Nuthall, 2007). Of course, this doesn't mean that this is the right place for them to be. One strategy to encourage students to embrace the space beyond their comfort zone – and in fact one of the most enjoyable things about teaching to the top – is to work to instil a culture of intellectual curiosity. Teachers can model the enthusiastic acquisition of knowledge by sharing *how* they learned something, for example: 'This is something I learned in my degree' or 'Actually, this is something I learned just last week, and it's really interesting because…'. So, as teachers, as well as modelling high-level knowledge, we can also model the right approach to take when confronted with new or challenging ideas: enthusiasm, interest and intellectual engagement. If students see you happily sharing your own route to learning, as well as enjoying using high-level concepts, they are more likely to enjoy using high-level knowledge themselves.

Motivation is also likely to be increased when students view their learning as having inherent value. Therefore, teachers should consider discussing the value of learning challenging concepts with the student body, for instance in assemblies. In this way, the importance and the value of academic knowledge can be reiterated beyond the classroom. Donohoo, Hattie and Eells (2018:44) suggest that if the 'narrative' of school life revolves around 'compliance to procedures', students will have an inevitably limited view of the purpose of schooling. By contrast, if the narrative centres on learning, high expectations and growth, students will 'think about learning in a different way. They will believe that learning is about challenge, about understanding and realising high expectations, and that setbacks are an opportunity to learn.' In other words, what are the messages we are delivering to students on a regular basis about the purpose of learning? Are they more likely to receive a lecture on school uniform policies in assembly, or an inspiring talk about the value of philosophy, the purpose of challenging one's own thinking and preconceptions, or an introduction to a key historical or contemporary thinker? These messages, on a whole school basis, make an impact when delivered consistently and thoughtfully.

Habitus, cultural capital and the confidence to reach for the top

Increasing students' confidence and academic self-concept may not only have ramifications for their achievement in a single subject or for their exam results, but I would suggest that it could also enable them to have confidence that reaches far beyond the school gates in the way in which they interact with the world. Bourdieu's concept of the *habitus* (1977) refers to the way in which our socially situated experiences are reproduced in the way in which we behave in and experience the world as individuals – in other words, how our social environment and experiences influence our identity. It also explains how, in society, we come to associate certain behaviours and ways of being with certain social groups. Part of the lack of comfort or self-confidence with certain types of knowledge may come partly from a social message that certain types of knowledge do not *belong* to certain students.

To use a personal example, my Grandad is a firmly working-class man who started his working life sticking labels on boxes in a factory and then worked in manual jobs such as caretaking for most of his life. He also loves opera and has a particular fondness for Puccini. When my working-class Grandad with his Cockney accent tells his acquaintances that his granddaughter is taking him to the opera they sometimes laugh out loud because, to them, it sounds so incongruous. Why should this be? Well, I think it is because we, unfortunately, live in a society where certain forms of knowledge and culture are largely deemed to only be the preserve of the middle and upper classes. The reason my Grandad doesn't mind breaking this stereotype is not that he was taught about opera at school or drummed in 'cultural capital'; he hated school and left early. The fact that he thinks nothing of reading a 600-page book on a historical event, debating the rights and wrongs of a political proposal, or developing an interest in opera after seeing *Madame Butterfly* once on the TV, is not down to the content of his curriculum 70 years ago. Instead, his ability to do these things comes from a strong sense of *confidence* and high academic self-concept. Somehow, despite being working class and leaving school at fourteen, he never received the memo that certain types of knowledge were off-limits to him. He doesn't feel inferior because he has always had the confidence to develop whatever interests he likes and to believe that no type of knowledge is inaccessible to him. I don't quite know where my Grandad's confidence comes from, but I do know that it means that his *habitus* does not restrict his life or interests. He is proud of the 'working class' elements of his identity but is also able to explore elements of the world that some people seem to think would be beyond it. By contrast, a student who asks 'Is there any point in this *for me?*' is demonstrating the opposite mindset. They are showing an internalised lack of confidence which feeds into a belief that certain forms of knowledge are both irrelevant and inaccessible.

Although the design of the curriculum to include higher-level knowledge at a challenging level is crucial, even more important is the way we develop students' self-esteem and their academic self-concept because this is far more likely to carry them effectively through life than a checklist of knowledge. So, although this might be surprising to readers considering the title of this book and many of the messages within it, ultimately the most significant benefit of teaching to the top lies in making students feel they deserve to access all levels of knowledge and to be confident in their interactions with the world in an academic sense. Anyone who feels that a certain type of knowledge is off-limits to them because of their grades or background has been taught or has learned that they deserve less. If they choose not to have an interest in something, this is a different matter, but often what we need to harness is students' self-belief and confidence in their own right to that knowledge.

It's not necessary for students to leave their own culture or identity behind and become someone who talks about the ballet at dinner parties – unless, of course, they want to. Bourdieu's (1986) notion of *cultural capital*, or the elements of a person's education (knowledge and intellectual skills) that provide a route to higher social status in society, has often been appropriated to suggest that we should drill students in a list of cultural knowledge to allow them access to the middle class. Since cultural capital provides 'the means for a non-economic form of domination and hierarchy, as classes distinguish themselves through taste' (Gaventa, 2003:6), the thinking goes that we should teach students a set list of 'cultural knowledge' in order to grant them access to social mobility. Yet as Phil Beadle persuasively argues in his book *The Fascist Painting*, the misunderstanding and misapplication of Bourdieu's notion of cultural capital can act as a form of 'symbolic violence' on the working class, rejecting their identity and asking them to 'worship the cultural tastes of their masters' (2020:225). Rather than just coming up with a list of cultural knowledge that students' 'should' know, if we increase students' confidence and academic concept alongside exposing them to a range of challenging concepts and high-level ideas, then we equip them to access whatever forms of culture or knowledge they wish to in their life beyond school. We do not suggest that any one form of cultural product is inherently preferable to another. However, we do open doors for them that they can walk through in the future, should they so choose.

QUESTIONS FOR REFLECTION

- How do you 'champion' the students in your classroom? Is there anything further you could do to champion them? What are the things that sometimes prevent this from happening?
- What are the dangers facing students' academic self-concept in your classroom and which aspects of this chapter could you apply to help students develop theirs?
- Think back to Deci and Ryan's self-determination triad of autonomy, competence and motivation. Could you increase any of these elements in your classroom, to help develop students' motivation to succeed? Which and why?
- Which of your students could particularly benefit from greater academic self-concept? Which strategies explored in this chapter would be most helpful for them?
- Is your classroom a safe space to take risks? In what ways could it be more so?
- How do you strike a balance between challenge and encouragement in your classroom? If you increase the level of challenge, how will you simultaneously increase the level of encouragement? What strategies will be most applicable in your subject?

Conclusion

'Hold fast to dreams
For if dreams die
Life is a broken-winged bird
That cannot fly.' – Langston Hughes

Aspiration for our students

The etymology of the verb 'aspire' is interesting. It comes from the Latin *aspirationem* which means 'breathing on; blowing upon', which later transmogrified into its use as a word meaning 'influence', 'strive for' and 'reach'. While 'aspire' is nowadays used in a medical sense as a synonym for breathing *in* rather than out, to my mind the initial linguistic meaning of 'breathing upon' makes perfect sense as a precursor to its more modern meaning of striving for a goal or ambition. Aspiration in both senses – of breathing out, and having ambition – suggests an externalisation and outward expression of something within us, or a pushing *outwards* of our inner ambitions and desires. Accordingly, when teaching to the top, we provide the space for students' aspirations to be expressed and enacted. We make space for them to strive, to 'breathe out', to externalise their potential, and to ensure that they perceive no ceiling on their ability.

I believe that aspiration is more important than anything else when it comes to student achievement and education. More important than subject knowledge, pedagogy and curriculum, because the aspirations we have for our students will ultimately underpin everything we do and the kind of teacher we become for them. Teaching to the top is all about aspiration and everything that I have explored in this book relies, fundamentally, on having high aspirations for our students. When we develop our subject knowledge, we show far-reaching aspirations for what our pupils deserve to learn. When we embed higher-level concepts and knowledge in our curricula and lesson planning, we are stating: 'We believe in our students.' When we build in opportunities for students to think deeply and to be challenged conceptually, we show the greatest of ambitions for what they are capable of. When we are brave enough to veer off-course in a lesson and explore an unexpected question or direction, we have faith in the high level of content our students are able to grapple with and we have high aspirations for their right to knowledge that goes beyond the curriculum. When we refuse to differentiate by task or assignment and instead set high expectations for all and support students to meet those expectations, we show ambition for all our students. When we work to make questioning more challenging, classroom talk more dialogic and exploratory, or give opportunities for creative expression, we show high aspirations for the way our students will be able to incorporate and critically consider challenging concepts in a plethora of contexts. And, when we devote time and energy to giving students the confidence and self-esteem to believe they can succeed, we show ambition for their right to high-level knowledge and demonstrate our commitment to empowering learners through challenging them intellectually.

The joy, value and challenge of teaching to the top doesn't only lie in aspiring highly for our students. It also lies in having high aspirations for ourselves. Alongside creating the conditions for students' aspirations, teaching to the top means having the highest of ambitions for our *own* development and subject knowledge. In turn, we need school leaders to have high aspirations for teachers' subject knowledge – including their own – and to provide space for this to be a fundamental part of staff development.

Creating space for success

The metaphor of *pushing* students to succeed is commonly used in discussions around challenge and teaching to the top in schools. However, I would suggest that it is entirely the wrong metaphor. It creates an impression of students as inert and passive objects who need to be driven, perhaps against their will, to the top. Instead, I think it is more helpful to think about teaching to the top as a way of giving students an insight into the intellectual heights they can reach and which are available to them, then providing room, space and support for them to reach those heights. I hope that I have conveyed in these pages that teaching to the top is not about pulling, cajoling, or dragging a child to achieve a certain grade or mark. It is a mindset that begins before we even set foot in the classroom. It is believing that all our students deserve access to higher-level ideas and it is thinking critically and carefully about how we can best translate these concepts to the classroom. It is setting the highest of goals for all, not for some.

Teaching to the top cannot be reduced to a narrow checklist of techniques. It doesn't mean valuing academic knowledge above all else. It's not about every teacher having an Oxbridge degree. It is not only about helping students to gain maximum progress or great examination results, although it certainly can aid us in achieving those aims. Essentially, teaching to the top means encouraging excitement for learning by demonstrating enthusiasm for higher-level concepts and giving students opportunities to think deeply, discuss difficult or challenging ideas, and become questioning and reflective learners. Teaching to the top is also, crucially, a belief that all students *deserve* to be taught about challenging concepts and ideas. It is an inclusive vision for social justice because when we teach to the top for every student, we empower all students to believe that they have the right to access any type of knowledge.

My broader vision is of an education system where teaching to the top is the norm in every classroom. A system where 'all, most, some' or other differentiated expectations are anathema to every teacher, and where teachers are given ample time and space for the development of their own subject knowledge. A system in which teachers feel confident in diverging from the lesson plan to explore avenues of intellectual curiosity and where they are trusted to exercise professional judgement in doing so. Where challenge is embedded in every aspect of curriculum planning, and where higher-level knowledge and academically challenging concepts are celebrated. Depending on the school in which you teach, you may face some structural, school-wide restrictions on your practice. In many cases, we are not there yet when it comes to teaching to the top in the education system as a whole. However, whatever school or system we work within, we can elicit change and make an immeasurable difference to the students in our classrooms simply by consistently teaching to the top, in every possible sense and at every possible opportunity. By aiming high for each one of our students, day in and day out, lesson after lesson. By aspiring to the highest levels of intellectual challenge at every turn.

If we want the very best for our students, teaching to the top is, quite simply, essential.

There is no other way.

References

Aflalo, E. (2021) 'Students generating questions as a way of learning', *Active Learning in Higher Education*, 22(1), pp. 63-75.

Alexander, R. J. (2006) *Towards Dialogic teaching: rethinking classroom talk* (3rd ed.). Cambridge: Dialogos.

Alexander, R. J. (2008) *Essays on Pedagogy*. London: Routledge.

Allington, R. L., Johnston, P. H. and Day, J. P. (2002) 'Exemplary fourth-grade teachers', *Language Arts,* 79, pp. 462-466.

Amemiya, J. and Wang, M. T. (2018) 'Why effort praise can backfire in adolescence', *Child Development Perspectives,* 12(3), pp. 199-203.

Aryana, M. (2010) 'Relationship between self-esteem and academic achievement amongst pre-university students', *Journal of Applied Sciences,* 10, pp. 2474-2477.

Bage, G., Grosvenor, J. and Williams, M. (1999) 'Curriculum planning: prediction or response? A case-study of teacher planning conducted through partnership action research', *The Curriculum Journal*, 10(1), pp. 49-69.

Bandura, A. (1993) 'Perceived selfefficacy in cognitive development and functioning', *Educational Psychologist,* 28(2), pp. 117-148.

Beadle, P. (2020) *The Fascist Painting: What is Cultural Capital?* Woodbridge: John Catt Educational.

Bjork, E. L. and Bjork, R. A. (2011) *Making things hard on yourself, but in a good way: Creating desirable difficulties to enhance learning.* In M. A. Gernsbacher, R. W. Pew, L. M. Hough, J. R. Pomerantz (Eds.) & FABBS Foundation, *Psychology and the real world: Essays illustrating fundamental contributions to society*, pp. 56-64. New York: Worth Publishers.

Bleiman, B. (2021) 'Dialogic Learning - More Than Just Talk'. *English and Media Centre Blog* [Blog] 12 April. Retrieved from: www.bit.ly/3xC6nOu

Bourdieu, P. (1977) *Outline of a Theory of Practice.* Cambridge: Cambridge University Press.

Bourdieu, P. (1986) *The Forms of Capital.* In J. Richardson (Ed.) *Handbook of Theory and Research for the Sociology of Capital*, pp. 241-58. New York: Greenwood Press.

Brown, P., Roediger, H. and McDaniel, M. (2014) *Make it stick: The science of successful learning.* Cambridge, MA: Harvard University Press.

Burbules, N. C. and Linn, M. C. (1988) 'Response to contradiction: Scientific reasoning during adolescence', *Journal of Educational Psychology,* 80(1), pp. 67-75.

Butler, A. C. (2010) 'Repeated testing produces superior transfer of learning relative to repeated studying', *Journal of Experimental Psychology: Learning, Memory, and Cognition,* 36(5), pp. 1118-1133.

Butler, R. (1988) 'Enhancing and undermining intrinsic motivation: The effects of task-involving and ego-evolving evaluation on interest and performance', *British Journal of Educational Psychology,* 58(1), pp. 1-14.

Byrne, B. (1990) 'Self-Concept and Academic Achievement: Investigating Their Importance as Discriminators of Academic Track Membership in High School', *Canadian Journal of Education,* 15(2), pp. 173-182.

Carter, R. (1990) *Knowledge about Language and the Curriculum: The LINC Reader.* London: Hodder.

Case, R. (2013) 'The unfortunate consequences of Bloom's taxonomy', *Social Education,* 77(4) pp. 196-200.

Caviglioli, O. (2019) *Dual Coding with Teachers.* Melton, Woodbridge: John Catt Educational.

Chamberlin, K., Yasué, M. and Chiang, I.-C. A. (2018) 'The impact of grades on student motivation', *Active Learning in Higher Education,* 14(2), pp. 149-61.

Chen, S., Yeh. Y., Hwang, F. and Lin, S. S. J. (2013) 'The relationship between academic self-concept and achievement: A multicohort-multioccasion study', *Learning and Individual Differences,* 23, pp. 172-178.

Chevalier, A., Gibbons, S., Thorpe, A., Snell, M. and Hoskins, S. (2009) 'Students' academic self-perception.' *Economics of Education Review,* 28(6), pp. 716-727.

Coe, R. (2013) *Improving Education: A triumph of hope over experience.* Inaugural Lecture of Professor Robert Coe, Durham University, 18 June 2013. Retrieved from: www.bit.ly/2T8AEFU

Coe, R., Aloisi, C., Higgins, S. and Major, L. E. (2014) 'What makes great teaching? Review of the underpinning research.' *The Sutton Trust Report.* Retrieved from: www.bit.ly/3wA6toK

Cohen, L., Manion, L. and Morrison, K. (2004) *A Guide to Teaching Practice.* London: Routledge.

Coleman, R. (2017) 'EEF Blog: The danger of oversimplifying the traditional vs progressive debate.' *The Education Endowment Foundation.* Blog post. Retrieved from: www.bit.ly/3ASNSYs

Cordingley, P., Bell, M., Rundell, B. and Evans, D. (2005) 'The impact of collaborative CPD on classroom teaching and learning', *Research Evidence in Education Library*. London: EPPICentre, Social Science Research Unit, Institute of Education. Retrieved from: www.bit.ly/3xB95Ea

Cremin, T. (2014) *Teaching English Creatively*. London: Routledge.

Csikszentmihalyi, M. (1990) *Flow*. New York: Harper and Row.

Cuccio-Schirripa, S. and Steiner, H. E. (2000) 'Enhancement and analysis of science question level for middle school students', *Journal of Research in Science Teaching*, 37, pp. 210-224.

Deci, E. L. (1971) 'Effects of externally mediated rewards on intrinsic motivation', *Journal of Personality and Social Psychology*, 18, pp. 105-115.

Deci, E. and Ryan, R. (2000) 'Intrinsic and Extrinsic Motivations: Classic Definitions and New Directions', *Contemporary Educational Psychology* 25, pp. 54-67.

Demie, F. and McLean, C. (2017) *Black Caribbean Underachievement in Schools in England*. London: Lambeth Education and Learning: Schools' Research and Statistics Unit. Retrieved from: www.bit.ly/3AMTFPb

Department for Education (2018) *Grants to pilot curriculum programmes in science, history and geography*. Retrieved from: www.bit.ly/3e9iATk

Department for Education (2019a) *The education inspection framework*. Retrieved from: www.bit.ly/3r4IZa1

Department for Education (2019b) *School inspection update*. Retrieved from: www.bit.ly/3r0yZyE

Didau, D. (2015) 'The problem with lesson planning.' *The Learning Spy* [Blog] 1 February. Retrieved from: www.bit.ly/3xuB7kB

Donohoo, J., Hattie, J. and Eells, R. (2018) 'The power of collective efficacy', *Educational Leadership*. 75, pp. 40-44.

Dudley-Marling, C. and Michaels, S. (2012) *High-Expectation Curricula: Helping All Students Succeed with Powerful Learning*. New York: Teachers College Press.

Dweck, C. S. (2008) *Mindset: the new psychology of success*. New York: Ballantine Books.

Educational Endowment Foundation (2020) 'Dialogic Teaching.' *EEF Project Report.*. Retrieved from: www.bit.ly/3xyHlA4

Educational Endowment Foundation (2021) 'Setting or Streaming', *The EEF Teaching and Learning Toolkit*. Retrieved from: www.bit.ly/3wxeUBe

Ellis, V. (2007) 'Taking subject knowledge seriously: from professional knowledge recipes to complex conceptualizations of teacher development', *The Curriculum Journal*, 18(4), pp. 447-462.

Eppley, K. and Dudley-Marling, C. (2019) 'Does direct instruction work?: A critical assessment of direct instruction research and its theoretical perspective', *Journal of Curriculum and Pedagogy*, 16(1), pp. 35-54.

Feshbach, N. D. and Feshbach, S. (2009) *Empathy and education*. In Decety, J. and Ickes, W. (Eds.), *Social neuroscience. The social neuroscience of empathy*, pp. 85-97. Cambridge, MA: MIT Press.

Firth, J., Smith, M., Harvard, B. and Boxer, A. (2017) 'Assessment as Learning: The Role of Retrieval Practice in the Classroom', *Impact: The Journal of the Chartered College of Teaching*. Retrieved from: www.bit.ly/3r3y40a

Fisher, D., Frey, N. and Hattie, J. (2017) *Visible learning for literacy, grades K-12: Implementing the practices that work best to accelerate student learning*. Thousand Oaks, CA: Corwin Press.

Fordham, N. W. (2006) 'Crafting questions that address comprehension strategies in content reading', *Journal of Adolescent and Adult Literacy*, 49(5), pp. 390-396.

Francis, B., Archer, L., Hodgen, J., Pepper, D., Taylor, B. and Travers, M-C. (2017) 'Exploring the relative lack of impact of research on 'ability grouping' in England: A discourse analytic account', *Cambridge Journal of Education*, 47(1), pp. 1-18.

Francis, B., Craig, N., Hodgen, J., Taylor, B., Tereshchenko, A., Connolly, P. and Archer, L. (2020) 'The impact of tracking by attainment on pupil self-confidence over time: demonstrating the accumulative impact of self-fulfilling prophecy.' *British Journal of Sociology of Education*, 41(5), pp. 626-642.

Freund, P. A. and Kasten, N. (2012) 'How smart do you think you are? A meta-analysis on the validity of self-estimates of cognitive ability', *Psychology Bulletin*, 138(2), pp. 296-321.

Gajda, A., Karwowski, M. and Beghetto, R. A. (2017) 'Creativity and academic achievement: A meta-analysis', *Journal of Educational Psychology*, 109, pp. 269-299.

Gaventa, J. (2003) *Power after Lukes: an overview of theories of power since Lukes and their application to development*. Brighton: Institute of Development Studies.

Gibb, N. (2017) 'The evidence in favour of teacher-led instruction'. Speech delivered 24th January 2017. Retrieved from: www.bit.ly/3yI3UlK

Gibbs, G. and Simpson, C. (2004) 'Conditions under which assessment supports students' learning', *Learning and Teaching in Higher Education*, 1, pp. 3-31.

Ginott, H. (1972) *Between Teacher and Child: A Book for Parents and Teachers*. New York: Scribner Book Company.

Giovanelli, M. (2015a) 'Becoming an English language teacher: linguistic knowledge, anxieties and the shifting sense of identity', *Language and Education*, 29(9), pp. 416-429.

Giovanelli, M. (2015b) *Teaching Grammar, Structure and Meaning: Exploring Theory and Practice for Post-16 English Language Teachers*. Oxford: Routledge.

Goddard, R. D. (2002) 'A theoretical and empirical analysis of the measurement of collective efficacy: The development of a short form', *Educational and Psychological Measurement*, 62(1), pp. 97-110.

Goddard, R. D., Hoy, W. K. and Woolfolk Hoy, A. (2004) 'Collective efficacy beliefs: Theoretical developments, empirical evidence, and future directions', *Educational Researcher*, 33(3), pp. 3-13.

Greenwald, A. and Krieger, L. (2006) 'Implicit bias: Scientific foundations', *California Law Review*, 94(4), pp. 945-967.

Guay, F., Marsh, H. W. and Boivin, M. (2003) 'Academic self-concept and academic achievement: Developmental perspectives on their causal ordering', *Journal of Educational Psychology*, 95(1), pp. 124-136.

Gunn, T. M. (2008) 'The effects of questioning on text processing', *Reading Psychology*, 29(5), pp. 405-442.

Haimovitz, K. and Dweck, C. S. (2017) 'The Origins of Children's Growth and Fixed Mindsets: New Research and a New Proposal', *Child Development*, 88(6), pp. 1849-1859.

Hamre, B. K. and Pianta, R. C. (2006) *Student-Teacher Relationships*. In G. G. Bear and K. M. Minke (Eds.), *Children's needs III: Development, prevention, and intervention*, pp. 59-71. Washington, DC: National Association of School Psychologists.

Harford, S. (2018) 'Assessment – what are inspectors looking at?', *Ofsted blog: schools, early years, further education and skills*. Retrieved from: www.bit. ly/2T74qLa

Harwell, S. H., Gunter, S., Montgomery, S., Shelton, C. and West, D. (2001) 'Technology integration and the classroom learning environment: research for action', *Learning Environments Research*, 4, pp. 259-286.

Hattie, J. (2009) *Visible Learning*. London: Routledge.

Hattie, J. (2011) *Visible Learning for Teachers*. London: Routledge.

Hattie, J. (2016) 'Third Annual Visible Learning Conference (subtitled Mindframes and Maximizers)', July 11 [Conference] Washington, D.C.

Haycock, K. (2006) *Improving achievement and closing gaps between groups*. Washington D.C: The Education Trust.

Hendrick, C. and Macpherson, R. (2017) *What Does This Look Like In The Classroom? Bridging The Gap Between Research And Practice.* Melton, Woodbridge: John Catt Educational.

Heritage, M. and Heritage, J. (2013) 'Teacher Questioning: The Epicenter of Instruction and Assessment', *Applied Measurement in Education,* 26(3), pp. 176-190.

Hirsch, Donald. (2007) *Chicken and Egg: Child Poverty and Educational Inequalities.* London: Child Poverty Action Group. Retrieved from: www. bit.ly/2UzAJCN

Howard, K. and Hill, C. (2020) *Symbiosis: The Curriculum and the Classroom.* Woodbridge: John Catt Educational.

Hunkins, F. P. (1989) *Teaching Thinking Through Effective Questioning.* Norwood, MA: Christopher Gordon Publishing Inc.

Hutchings, M. (2015) 'Exam Factories?: The Impact of Accountability Measures on Children and Young People: Research Commissioned by the National Union of Teachers.' *Communications Department of The National Union of Teachers.*

Immordino-Yang, M. H. (2016) *Emotions, Learning, and the Brain: Exploring the Educational Implications of Affective Neuroscience.* New York: W. W. Norton & Co.

Immordino-Yang, M. H. and Damasio, A. R. (2007) 'We feel, therefore we learn: the relevance of affective and social neuroscience to education', *Mind, Brain and Education,* 1(1), pp. 3-10.

Ireson, J. and Hallam, S. (2001) *Ability Grouping in Education.* London: Paul Chapman Publishing.

Jackson, C. (2010) 'Fear in Education', *Educational Review,* 62(1), pp. 39-52.

Johnson, J. (1994) 'The National Oracy Project'. In S. Brindley (Ed.) *Teaching English,* pp. 29-30. London: Routledge.

John, P. D. (2006) 'Lesson planning and the student teacher: re-thinking the dominant model', *Journal of Curriculum Studies,* 38(4), pp. 483-498.

Kahneman, D. (2011) *Thinking, Fast and Slow.* London: Penguin.

Karwowski, M., Jankowska, D. M., Brzeski, A., Czerwonka, M., Gajda, A., Lebuda, I. and Beghetto, R. A. (2020) 'Delving into Creativity and Learning', *Creativity Research Journal,* 32(1), pp. 4-16.

Khairudin, R., Nasir, R., Halim, F., Zainah, A., Wan Shahrazad, W. S., Ismail, K. and Valipour, G. M. (2012) 'Emotion and explicit verbal memory: evidence using Malay Lexicon', *Asian Social Science* 8(38).

King, A. (1989) 'Effects of self-questioning training on college students' comprehension of lectures', *Contemporary Educational Psychology,* 14, pp. 366-381.

Kirby, P. and Cullinane, C. (2016) 'Class differences: ethnicity and disadvantage', *Research brief for the Sutton Trust*. Retrieved from: www.bit.ly/36wR1Pr

Lakoff, G. and Johnson, M. (1980) *Metaphors We Live By*. Chicago, IL: The University of Chicago Press.

Leach, J. and Moon, B. (2000) 'Pedagogy, information and communications technology and teachers' professional knowledge', *The Curriculum Journal*, 11(3), pp. 384-404.

Lefebvre, H. (1991) *The Production of Space*. Oxford: Blackwell.

Lewin, L. (2010) 'Teaching critical reading with questioning strategies', *Educational Leadership*, 67(6). Retrieved from: www.bit.ly/2T3Db42

Mac an Ghaill, M. (1988) *Young, gifted and black: Student–teacher relations in the schooling of black youth*. Milton Keynes: Open University Press.

Maisuria, A. (2005) 'The Turbulent Times of Creativity in the National Curriculum', *Policy Futures in Education*, 32(2), pp. 141-152.

Mansworth, M. (2016) 'Creative Potential Within Policy: An Analysis of the 2013 English Literature Curriculum', *English in Education*, 50(1), pp. 116-129.

Markus, H. and Kunda, Z. (1986) 'Stability and Malleability of the Self Concept.' Journal of Personality and Social Psychology, 51(4), pp. 858-66.

Marsh, H. W. and Craven, R. G. (2006) 'Reciprocal effects of self-concept and performance from a multidimensional perspective: Beyond seductive pleasure and unidimensional perspectives', *Perspectives on Psychological Science*, 1, pp. 133-163.

Mason, J. and Giovanelli, M. (2021) *Studying Fiction: A Guide for Teachers and Students*. London: Routledge.

McNamara, D. (1991) 'Subject Knowledge and its Application: problems and possibilities for teacher educators.' *Journal of Education for Teaching*, 17(2), pp. 113-128.

Mercer, N. (2019) *Language and the Joint Creation of Knowledge: The Selected Works of Neil Mercer*. London: Routledge.

Mercer, N., Dawes, L., Wegerif, R. and Sams, C. (2004) 'Reasoning as a scientist: ways of helping children to use language to learn science', *British Educational Research Journal*, 30(3), pp. 359-377.

Meta, J. and Fine, S. (2019) *In search of deeper learning*. Cambridge, MA: Harvard University Press.

Mueller, C. M. and Dweck, C. S. (1998) 'Praise for intelligence can undermine children's motivation and performance', *Journal of Personality and Social Psychology*, 75(1), pp. 33-52.

Muijs, R. D. and Reynolds, D. (2002) 'Teacher Beliefs and Behaviours: What really matters?', *Journal of Classroom Interaction*, 37(2), pp. 3-15.

Murayama, K., Pekrun, R., Suzuki, M., Marsh, H. W. and Lichtenfeld, S. (2016) 'Don't aim too high for your kids: Parental overaspiration undermines students' learning in mathematics.' *Journal of Personality and Social Psychology*, 111(5), pp. 766-779.

Musanti, S. and Pence, L. (2010) 'Collaboration and Teacher Development: Unpacking Resistance, Constructing Knowledge, and Navigating Identities', *Teacher Education Quarterly*, 37(1), pp. 73-89.

Myatt, M. (2018) *The Curriculum: Gallimaufry to coherence*. Melton, Woodbridge: John Catt Educational.

Myatt, M. (2020) *Back on Track: Fewer things, great depth*. Melton, Woodbridge: John Catt Educational.

Nicol, D. J. (2010) 'From monologue to dialogue: improving written feedback processes in mass higher education', *Assessment and Evaluation in Higher Education*, 35(5), pp. 501-517.

Nuthall, G. (2007) *The Hidden Lives of Learners*. Wellington: New Zealand Council for Educational Research Press.

Patrick, B. C., Hisley, J. and Kempler, T. (2000) 'What's Everybody So Excited About?: The Effects of Teacher Enthusiasm on Student Intrinsic Motivation and Vitality', *The Journal of Experimental Education*, 68(3), pp. 217 236.

Paul, R. and Elder, L. (2008) 'Critical Thinking: The Art of Socratic Questioning: Part III', *Journal of Developmental Education*, 31(3), pp. 34-36..

Pierson, R. (2013) 'Every child needs a champion', *TED Talks Education*. Retrieved from: www.bit.ly/3e8Dsde

Rawling, E. and Westaway, J. (2003) 'Exploring creativity', *Teaching Geography*, pp. 5-8.

Reynolds, D. and Farrell, S. (1996) *Worlds apart? A review of international surveys of educational achievement involving England*. London: Her Majesty's Stationery Office.

Robinson, M. (2013) *Trivium 21c: Preparing young people for the future with lessons from the past*. Carmarthen, Wales: Independent Thinking Press.

Roediger, H. L., McDermott, K. B. and McDaniel, M. A. (2011) *Using testing to improve learning and memory*. In M. A. Gernsbacher, R. Pew, L. Hough and J. R. Pomerantz (Eds.), *Psychology and the real world: Essays illustrating fundamental contributions to society*, pp. 65-74. New York: Worth Publishing Co.

Rogers, C. (1959) 'A theory of therapy, personality and interpersonal relationships as developed in the client-centered framework.' In S. Koch (Ed.), *Psychology:*

A study of a science. Vol. 3: Formulations of the person and the social context. New York: McGraw Hill.

Rohrer, D. and Taylor, K. (2007) 'The shuffling of mathematics practice problems improves learning', *Instructional Science,* 35, pp. 481-498.

Roman, S., Cuestas, P. J. and Fenollar, P. (2008) 'An examination of the interrelationships between self-esteem, others' expectations, family support, learning approaches and academia achievement', *Studies in Higher Education,* 33, pp. 127-138.

Roorda, D. L., Koomen, H., Spilt, J. L, and Oort, F. J. (2011) 'The Influence of Affective Teacher–Student Relationships on Students' School Engagement and Achievement: A Meta-Analytic Approach', *Review of Educational Research,* 81(4), pp. 493-529.

Rosenshine, B. (1970) 'Enthusiastic teaching: A research review', *The School Review,* 78(4), pp. 499-515.

Rosenthal, R. and Jacobson, L. (1968) *Pygmalion in the classroom: teacher expectation and pupils' intellectual development.* New York: Holt, Rinehart and Winston.

Rubie-Davies, C. M. (2006) 'Teacher Expectations and Student Self-Perceptions: Exploring Relationships', *Psychology in the Schools,* 43(5), pp. 537-552.

Sanchez, H. S. (2014) 'The impact of self-perceived subject matter knowledge on pedagogical decisions in EFL grammar teaching practices', *Language Awareness,* 23(3), pp. 220-233.

Saxe, G. B., Gearhart, M. and Nasir, N. S. (2001) 'Enhancing students' understanding of mathematics: a study of three contrasting approaches to professional support', *Journal of Mathematics Teacher Education,* 4, pp. 55-79.

Sinclair, J. and Coulthard, M. (1975) *Toward an analysis of discourse: the English used by teachers and pupils.* Oxford: Oxford University Press.

Siraj-Blatchford, I., Muttock, S., Sylva, K., Gilden, R. and Bell, D. (2002) *Researching effective pedagogy in the early years.* Research report for the Department for Education and Skills (DfES). London: Institute of Education.

Sherrington, T. (2014) 'The Progressive-Traditional Pedagogy Tree', *teacherhead* [Blog] 15 March. Retrieved from: www.bit.ly/3r5r6bd

Sherrington, T. (2017) *The Learning Rainforest.* Melton, Woodbridge: John Catt Educational.

Sherrington, T. and Caviglioli, O. (2020) *Teaching WalkThrus: Five Step Guides to Instructional Coaching.* Melton, Woodbridge: John Catt Educational.

Shulman, L. S. (1986) 'Those who understand: Knowledge growth in teaching', *Educational Researcher,* 15, pp. 4-14.

Shulman, L. S. (1987) 'Knowledge and teaching: Foundations of the new reform', *Harvard Educational Review*, 57, pp. 1-22.

Shulman, L. S. and Shulman, J. H. (2004) 'How and what teachers learn: a shifting perspective', *Journal of Curriculum Studies*, 36(2), pp. 257-271.

Simon, B. and Taylor, J. (2009) 'What is the value of course-specific learning goals?', *Journal of College Science Teaching*, 39, pp. 52-57.

Smagorinsky, P. (2018) 'Is Instructional Scaffolding Actually Vygotskian, and Why Should It Matter to Literacy Teachers?', *Journal of Adolescent & Adult Literacy*, 62(3), pp. 253-257.

Stockard, J., Wood T. W., Coughlin, C., Rasplica, Khoury C. (2018) 'The Effectiveness of Direct Instruction Curricula: A Meta-Analysis of a Half Century of Research', *Review of Educational Research*, 88(4), pp. 479-507.

Taylor, B., Francis, B., Archer, L., Hodgen, J., Pepper, D., Tereshchenko, A. and Travers, M-C. (2016) 'Factors deterring schools from mixed attainment teaching practice', *Pedagogy, Culture & Society*, 25(3), pp. 327-345.

Tiedemann, J. (2000) 'Parents' gender stereotypes and teachers' beliefs as predictors of children's concept of their mathematical ability in elementary school', *Journal of Educational Psychology*, 92(1), pp. 144-151.

Tripp, D. (1993) *Critical Incidents in Teaching*. London: Routledge.

Tyng, C. M., Amin, H. U., Saad, M. and Malik, A. (2017) 'The Influences of Emotion on Learning and Memory', *Frontiers in Psychology*, 8(1454), pp. 1-22.

Van Gog, T. and Sweller, J. (2015) 'Not new, but nearly forgotten: The testing effect decreases or even disappears as the complexity of learning materials increases', *Educational Psychology Review*, 27(2), pp. 247-264.

Vygotsky, L. S. and Cole, M., John-Steiner, V., Scribner, S. and Souberman, E. (Eds. and Trans.) (1978) *Mind in society: The development of higher psychological processes*. Cambridge, MA: Harvard University Press.

Wang, X., Su, Y., Cheung, S., Wong, E. and Kwong, T. (2013) 'An exploration of Biggs' constructive alignment in course design and its impact on students' learning approaches', *Assessment & Evaluation in Higher Education*, 38, pp. 477-491

Webb, J. (2019) *How to teach English literature: Overcoming cultural poverty*. Melton, Woodbridge: John Catt Educational.

Wenger, E. (1998) *Communities of Practice*. Cambridge: Cambridge University Press.

Wiliam, D. (2019) 'Teaching not a research-based profession'. *TES Online* [Website] 30 May. Retrieved from: www.bit.ly/2VCqtdH

Wilkinson, H., Putwain, D. and Mallaburn, A. (2020) 'How do teachers communicate to students about forthcoming GCSE exams?: An observational study', *The Psychology of Education Review*, 44(2), pp. 61-67.

Willingham, D. T. (2008) 'Critical Thinking: Why Is It So Hard to Teach?', *Arts Education Policy Review*, 109(4), pp. 21-32.

Worth, J. and Van den Brande, J. (2020) *Teacher autonomy: how does it relate to job satisfaction and retention?* Slough: NFER. Retrieved from: www.bit.ly/2TSezMf

Zazkis, R., Liljedahl, P. and Sinclair, N. (2009) Lesson Plays: Planning Teaching versus Teaching Planning. *For the Learning of Mathematics*, 29(1), pp. 40-47. Retrieved from www.bit.ly/2VzJHR1

Zenasni, F., Besançon, M. and Lubart, T. (2008) 'Creativity and Tolerance of Ambiguity: An Empirical Study', *The Journal of Creative Behaviour*. 42(1), pp. 61-73.

Zull, J. E. (2006) 'Key aspects of how the brain learns'. In S. Johnson & K. Taylor (Eds.), *The neuroscience of adult learning*, pp. 3-9. San Francisco: Jossey-Bass.